Also by Michael D. Kurtz:

Everyday Life in the Times of the Judges—Included in Abingdon's Bible Teacher Kit

Approaching the New Millennium: Biblical End-Time Images

Lessons from a Christmas Tree Farm: A Devotional and Study Guide Resource

CROSSINGS

MEMOIRS OF A MOUNTAIN MEDICAL DOCTOR

ELAM S. KURTZ, MD;
MICHAEL D. KURTZ, D. MIN

iUniverse, Inc.
New York   Bloomington

Crossings
Memoirs of a Mountain Medical Doctor

iUniverse books may be ordered through booksellers or by contacting:

iUniverse
1663 Liberty Drive
Bloomington, IN 47403
www.iuniverse.com
1-800-Authors (1-800-288-4677)

Because of the dynamic nature of the Internet, any Web addresses or links contained in this book may have changed since publication and may no longer be valid. The views expressed in this work are solely those of the author and do not necessarily reflect the views of the publisher, and the publisher hereby disclaims any responsibility for them.

ISBN: 978-1-4502-6246-0 (sc)
ISBN: 978-1-4502-6247-7 (ebook)

Printed in the United States of America

iUniverse rev. date: 10/21/2010

TO THE PEOPLE OF ASHE COUNTY, NORTH CAROLINA, WHO WELCOMED DR. ELAM KURTZ INTO THEIR HEARTS AND INTO THEIR LIVES, BEGINNING THE SUMMER OF 1956 AND CONTINUING WITH THIS SAME LOVE AND FAVOR UNTIL HIS DEATH—MONDAY, APRIL 26, 2010.

FOREWORD

Crossings have been a part of life as long as humankind has existed. History is replete with significant crossings. Israel crossed the Red Sea. Then it took them forty years to cross the wilderness before crossing the Jordan River. Hannibal crossed the Alps. Washington crossed the Delaware. Colonial pioneers crossed America.

Crossings enable us to get from one point to another. Crossings then become venues and pathways through which we navigate our journey. We must choose our crossings wisely and with great care for these decisions and choices determine our destination. In the spirit and words of American poet Robert Frost, "I chose the road less travelled and it has made all the difference since."

A crossing may be a literal geographical, physical crossing, whether mountain, sea, or desert. In addition, a crossing may be mental, emotional or spiritual in nature. Phases, stages and significant experiences bring these developmental and experiential crossings our way. Crossings, changes and transitions, breed angst and anxiety within us, for they represent unchartered territory in our lives; yet, they also offer the wonderful opportunity for novel exploration, new possibilities, and for new growth to become reality.

May "CROSSINGS: Memoirs of a Mountain Medical Doctor" provide one avenue of encouragement and inspiration for any and all changes, transitions, and crossings that you, the reader, encounter. May you be guided to wise choices and exciting adventures both as you read this book and as you navigate life.

INTRODUCTION

CROSSINGS: Memoirs of a Mountain Medical Doctor

Dr. Elam S. Kurtz was a man of great vision, a man of deep faith, and a man of enormous energy. With these qualities, and more, God formed, fashioned, and refined a person, and a medical doctor, who had a profound, and pervasive positive influence upon the many people whom his life touched and whom he served.

To his patients he was known as Dr. Kurtz, or "Doc." To his friends he was referred to as Elam. His family addressed him as Dad, or, in later years we affectionately labeled him "Pop".

Pop's eighty-six years of life yielded numerous transitions and changes in various areas and aspects of his living, or "crossings" as Dad referred to these transitions. This book attempts to capture and share many of these crossings. Yet, more than relating just the actual crossings, the hope is that readers will discover in these pages inspiration and motivation for their own journey crossings. By reflecting upon how one of God's children-- Elam S. Kurtz--embraced the transitions and crossings of life with great vision, deep faith, and enormous energy, may we also learn, and put into practice, the great lessons of life, seeking to serve God and humankind with our very best.

The writing that follows is laid out in six chapters. Each chapter follows a particular crossing, or transition topic, in Pop's journey. Chapter one looks at his primary and foundational crossing--theological crossings. Pop's Christian faith and values provided both the plumb line which tested and guided his choices and the lens through which he viewed all of life. Chapter two considers the many educational crossings throughout Dad's life. In chapter three we look at Pop's vocational crossings. And, in chapter four we explore the topic of relational and family crossings. Chapter five takes up the subject of geographical crossings. Finally, chapter six presents Dad's final crossing, reminding us that death is a part of life.

Pop took a pioneer posture to life. That is, he approached life with a spirit of exploration and great expectation. As with any pioneer Dad's stance and spirit necessitated moving, exploring, changing and adjusting--geographically, emotionally, intellectually and spiritually. For Pop, life was not static. Rather, life was dynamic and ever-changing. From his perspective life was an adventure filled with changes and crossings, to discover daily, in contrast to an existence to be merely tolerated or endured.

By definition, to be human mandates the encountering of transitions and changes. All persons face crossings. Life is constantly and continually changing. The lyrics of a particular song say it well: "The only thing that's permanent is change."

Some resist these changes. Some are re-active in the face of transitions. Some are passive when meeting life's crossings.

Some changes, to be sure, were difficult for Pop. Some transitions for him, like for all of us, he did not handle so well. And, some life crossings were tough for Dad to decide and discern. But this Pop taught by his lifestyle, to those who observed, he was pro-active as he faced life's crossings. He embraced life. He made the most of changes and transitions. Life for, and with, Pop was an adventure.

One further note about this memoir: Over the final three or four years of his life, Dad was actively doing research, taking notes, and attempting to collect and integrate various pieces of information and history to be placed into a book titled "Crossings." Dad was good at formulating the ideas. He had the vision. But a writer Dad was not. He had accumulated a lot of material but it lacked organization and it lacked unity and clarity. Pop had attempted to get a number of persons to assist him in getting the writing project completed but it always seemed, for whatever reasons, to be met with dead ends. So, after learning of his dilemma, in February of 2010, I expressed to Dad that I would help him with this book writing project. He was visibly relieved and expressed great gratitude that finally a plan was in place.

I am both humbled and honored by this writing task of remembering and reflecting upon Pop's life. Much of the content that follows includes and reflects Dad's research and in some cases his very own words and expressions. I have tried as best I could to include the major topics and writings that he stressed and highlighted. Fortunately, before he died Dad and I had some opportunities to discuss this writing. In one of those conversations we discussed the various chapter themes that comprise this book. Unfortunately, I did not have the many additional book discussion sessions for which we had planned and hoped. It was not to be. For on April 26th, 2010 Dad passed from this life into the next.

I consider this earthly loss of Dad to be an unanticipated and difficult crossing, an unexpected transition that came too early. Yet, in true Pop fashion, I hope and pray that, "CROSSINGS: Memoirs of a Mountain Medical Doctor," will encourage and enable others to approach life, and the plethora of changes and crossings that life brings, with renewed vision, increased faith, and unabated enthusiasm.

Michael D. Kurtz, D. Min.
May 2010

CONTENTS

CHAPTER ONE

THEOLOGICAL CROSSINGS

"God calls each generation to pass down spiritual truth to the next." -Dennis Rainey

---

Elam S. Kurtz was raised in a strong and supportive Christian home. He was brought up by parents Christian and Elsie Kurtz who taught him and his six siblings, prayers, scripture, hymns, and daily discipleship in Christ's name.

At age fourteen, Dad made a conscious choice to follow Jesus Christ as his Savior and Lord. This decision was symbolized and publically declared through his Christian baptism. Dad writes, "I perceived my need to be baptized at age ten, but did not yield to this conviction until several years later. At age fourteen I was baptized, along with a class of ten baptismal candidates, by the pouring of water by Bishop John S. Mast, and Deacon Sylvanus Stoltzfus. I recall that Deacon Stoltzfus urged us to ask for the Holy Spirit as we received water baptism."

For Pop religion was neither, Christianity by osmosis nor automatic religious succession through his parents. Rather, he had to take and make his own theological and spiritual crossing--a crossing enabled by Christ's amazing grace, transforming him from saintless-sinner to sinnered-saint.

Yet, for Pop, Christian conversion signified by baptism was in many ways just a beginning to a lifelong of discipleship and service to God and humankind. This discipleship and service for Dad was guided by the Holy Spirit, the Holy Scriptures, and the Body of Christ, the church. The Bible was his primary written source and guide. The scriptures were considered a love letter from God, providing providential guidance in the context of a divine-human relationship--divinely inspired words that called not only for intellectual ascent, but, in addition, volitional consent.

1

Following Dad's death the family located Pop's written response to the question, "What scriptural principles guide your life?" Pop replied with three principles:

1. "Whatsoever Thy hand findeth to do, do it with all Thy might." Ecclesiastes 9:10
2. "In all Thy ways acknowledge Him and He shall direct Thy paths." Proverbs 3:6
3. Changes come but one anchor endures: A life built upon the person of Jesus Christ. This later principle was no doubt a reference to I Corinthians 3:10, a signature scripture for Anabaptist reformer Menno Simons.

As Pop's above listed principles for living indicate, he very much promoted and embraced an active, pragmatic faith--a practical divinity. Dad espoused a philosophy and lived a lifestyle which adhered to the phrase, "Practice what you preach," or, again, "You shall know them by their fruit."

According to Dad's theology, not only should one's beliefs and Christian doctrine be practical and lived out and demonstrated in every day kind of ways; but, it should also affect and direct every area and aspect of a person's life. Thus, not only did Dr. Kurtz practice holistic medicine, he also sought to practice holistic living by example.

The Great Commandment Elam took to heart and practice. "Love the Lord your God with all your heart, mind and soul and love your neighbor as yourself" (Matthew 22:36-40). This sacred Commandment was much more than just words on a page for Dad. It was, rather, a directive for living.

A holistic approach to living acknowledges and celebrates God created all of life and God cares about all aspects of living--body, mind, and soul. This holistic, integrated view is the biblical, Judeo-Christian perspective on life, as contrasted with the segmented and divided philosophy of life maintained by the ancient Greeks.

The Hebrew-Christian scriptures support and affirm Creator God did not create human beings as one-dimensional. Instead, humans are created multi-dimensional--body, mind, and soul. And, furthermore, each dimension is worthy of attention and care; and, each portion has impact and influence upon all other parts in an interrelated, interdependent relationship.

Reflection upon, and observation of, Elam Kurtz's life evidenced a life of seemingly inexhaustible energy and activity in the holistic areas of body, mind and soul. In the area of bodily health, Dr. Kurtz stayed physically active until literally the last day of his life, giving attention to physical exercise and care of "the temple of the Holy Spirit," whether hiking the local mountains, biking the mountain roads, or in more recent years working out at Mountain Hearts Rehabilitation Center at Ashe Memorial Hospital in Jefferson, North Carolina.

As a Family Physician "Doc" Kurtz emphasized and concentrated upon the holistic care of his patients, mindful and inclusive of all areas of their life. Of course, as any good medical doctor, he attended to the presenting physical need. But, his belief in and commitment to holistic health caused him to look behind and beyond just the physical, to the totality of a person's life.

This pursuit of holistic patient care was evidenced, for example, in Dr. Kurtz's participation in, and advocacy of, mental health boards and agencies. Helping provide and insure adequate mental health care and resources for Ashe County citizens was a top priority for Dr. Kurtz. In preserved memoirs he reflects:

"Our Ashe County Mental Health Board travelled on one occasion to the University of Wisconsin for training with inter-disciplinary groups that inspired every participant and included resourceful presenters. University faculty assisted as well as the National Institute of Mental Health personnel. Participants came from all across the United States, representing metropolitan areas, as well as small rural communities. A variety of professions were represented including, university employees, governmental employees, nurses, social workers, and physicians. This diverse and varied participation afforded a rich milieu for 'cross-fertilization' as all learned from one another.

The center of attention was services for rural America. Out of this historic and watershed Conference there was formed a National Association for Rural Mental Health, which continues to this day. Most of the latest activity in North Carolina is based at the University of North Carolina at Chapel Hill.

Locally, I invited my medical students to attend the New River Mental Health Board meetings when timely. I also provided intentional time with my students to discuss office and hospital case studies to ensure that comprehensive care was provided. This seemed especially necessary and appropriate as no psychiatric consultants were available in our area.

It is vitally important that Family Practice physicians replace retiring physicians and keep up the special need caring and even add additional skills and responsibilities. They continue, for instance, to support traumatic stress victims, substance abuse, spouse abuse, compulsive disorders, phobias, anxiety, delayed grief with conversion reactions, child-molestation and the increase in dementias.

The 'new' breed of Family Physicians are now for the aging population not only counselors but also neurologists, cardiologists, gerontologists, and the primary specialist in each of these specialties, calling together an array of super-specialists but defining how much of any are desirable for each client. After the case has a solution the follow up remains to be both interpreted and faithfully managed. Certainly the Family Physician has filled a much-needed niche and made a significant 'crossing.'"

In keeping with a practice of holistic theology and lifestyle, Dr. Kurtz consistently and continually kept his "mental wheels turning" through reading, continuing education events and correspondence studies, which will be discussed more thoroughly in the next chapter. Whether as an advocate for New River Mental Health, reading one of the numerous volumes in his personal library, or staying current with the latest in medical practice, "Doc" continued employing and engaging his mind, and supporting and enabling positive mental health resources for others, until the very end of his life.

As important as physical exercise and stewardship of the body was for Pop; and, as crucial as right thinking and cognitive development was to him, that aspect of holistic thought which he valued most and which gave him vision and energy for life was soul care. To care for the body yields benefit. To develop the mind is commendable. But, to care for the soul was essential in Dad's theology and thinking. For soul care not only breeds abundant life here and now, but also yields eternal life forever and ever. For Dad, as for every follower of Jesus, the road of soul care follows the path of Jesus Christ. As Pop shared in his scripturally derived principles for living, "Changes come but one anchor endures: A life built upon the person of Jesus Christ." At another point in Pop's memoirs he records: "All true believers put Christ first. He is Author of our peace; Hope of our future; and, Inspiration of our lives." When Dad was asked on one occasion, "What advice about life do you want others to remember?" he responded with, "Whatever life brings, the central focus and the central person is Jesus."

Jesus is often referred to as the prince of peace. A central tenet of the Christian faith is peace. And, a foundational thread of Dad's theology was a nonresistant, peace position. He was raised in the Mennonite Church, a denomination and pietistic branch of Christianity that teaches and advances nonviolent pacifism in all relationships and contexts. About the Mennonites Dad explains: "The founders of the Mennonites in 1525 were called 're-baptizers' for rejecting the State Churches' acquiring their membership by infant baptism. Such opposing groups were fiercely persecuted and also arose not only in Switzerland but simultaneously on the Netherlands. The leadership and teaching publications came from Menno Simons in the Friesland. Hence, they obtained the name Mennonite. Only by confession of one's own faith could an applicant be baptized and then also gain entry as a member of the church. Evidence of the faith came from fruit bearing ('By their deeds you will know them').

Because the Mennonites believed following Christ entailed renouncing violence, life-giving and not life-taking, their refusal to take up arms threatened the sword-bearing state authorities. Often their citizenship, property ownership, and very lives were threatened. Their peace stance required paying a high price."

When asked to list what he considered to be his spiritual strengths, the very first item on Pop's list was "A promoter of peace." In fact, many of us recall how Dad would end his e-mails and writings with "shalom," the Hebrew term for peace. Shalom indicates a very comprehensive and nurturing type of peace, far more than merely the absence of war and conflict. Rather, it describes a peace which embraces and enhances justice, mercy and compassion.

Both as a person and as a physician Dad sought to bring shalom to those with whom he related and treated. Shalom, then, to Pop, was more than a greeting. It was a practice and a posture toward living. At one point Pop told his grandson Joshua, "Your one grandfather represents grace. Your other grandfather represents peace." Dad's grace reference was made out of deep respect for Rev. John Christy, Joshua's maternal grandfather, a man who truly embodied God's amazing grace. And, in the peace reference he was lifting up his own theological emphasis.

Upon the deep convictions and sound theology of, among others, Jesus as Savior and Lord; holistic Christian living; and, shalom, Dad planted his theological flag. These faith tenets kept him grounded.

However, a growing, vibrant faith and theology, and application of this theology, is never static. Of course, there are bedrock foundations and convictions from which one does not waiver; but, there are necessary and mandatory theological crossings and changes for the person on a Christian adventure. On one occasion the great reformer John Wesley affirmed: "In essentials, unity; In non-essentials, liberty; In all things, charity." Dad seemed to adhere to this philosophy, especially as he seasoned and matured in his Christian faith walk. He was raised in a culture that was considered by many to be rigid and strict, especially in terms of religious life. As Dad's Christian faith evolved and deepened he became more assured of God's grace and mercy. On this "grace transformation" Dad shares, "At Eastern

Mennonite College in short term Bible study I began to understand the in-dwelling of Christ in a person's life. Later, during the Cleveland, Ohio years, amongst a caring fellowship of believers, I accepted faith in Christ Jesus as contrasted with abiding in rules. Then, while teaching Sunday school years later I accepted the Hebrews, chapter 6, concept of the Most Holy Place, with the temple of God graciously located within me. Therein is my 'eternal security.' No need every night on returning to fear lest a sin should have been unnamed for forgiveness."

Dad's theological crossings, especially later in life, included moving away from a more rigid, performance-based doctrinal stance to a more open and grace-filled posture. As discussed earlier, without straying from his central and basic convictions and the foundational tenets of the Christian faith, Dad also was able to practice a gracious open-mindedness. This balanced and more diplomatic approach permitted him to more readily impact and influence the culture of which he had joined. This openness enabled a give and take style with others, which provided a more relational approach.

A primary example of this relational, balanced, and grace-based theology and practice was Pop's willingness to become an associate member of a local United Methodist Church, while at the same time maintaining membership at a local Mennonite Church. This integration of two primary and critical biblical and theological emphases--grace and peace--from two Christian denominations--United Methodist and Mennonite--provides just one illustration of Pop's theological transitions and crossings.

Dad wrote a letter to his parents on one occasion which evidences and expresses his dialog with, openness to, and appreciation of the spiritual life and style of the Ashe County folk. Excerpts of this letter include:

> Dear Papa and Mama,
> The people of this County have a rich spiritual heritage. They are closer to the Bible in their thinking than average American communities. They respect persons who follow Christ and especially appreciate it in their physicians. And, all the staff physicians at Ashe Hospital are church goers and supportive of the Christian walk.
> Secondly, their way of life is simplicity and disdain of the vain polish of which I also hate.
> Thirdly, I believe I have shown the community that I can transcend denominational lines when, for example, I am unable to attend my church of choice and instead

visit local churches near the hospital when I am on call. I have found I can contribute and dialog without carrying a denominational chip, but with readiness and kindness sharing my own convictions.

On a professional basis, I see my acceptance stemming from these sources: a desire to explain the processes of health and illness, the good graces of my mentor, Dr. Jones, and our participation in visiting in the homes of our mountain folk.

My prayer continues to be to harm no one; but instead to be always helpful, to be hopeful, and to be healthful.

Love,
Elam

Dad's relationship with Jesus Christ--the Author of grace and peace--was the driving force in his life. His decisions and choices were guided by his Christian faith. In the midst of his theological struggles, challenges and changes, there remained a rock-solid center. Once again in returning to Pop's own words, this foundation and central focus is affirmed, "Changes come but one anchor endures: A life built upon the person of Jesus Christ."

CHAPTER TWO
EDUCATIONAL CROSSINGS

"Education as growth or maturity should be an ever-present process." - Dewey

For Dad, education, both formal and informal, was a blessed privilege and a continual process. It was a privilege and blessing in that he considered education an opportunity that does not befall everyone, and should not, therefore, be taken for granted. And, he was convicted that education was a continual process that for the inquiring, open mind never ends.

The pursuit of the formal educational pathway was neither easy nor a straight line for Dad. There were turns, roadblocks and barriers along the way. As he shares, "I didn't have the opportunity all my siblings had to get a high school education. But the determination to get that education, which I did by home study, changed the status for all subsequent six siblings.

In addition, there were other challenges. For example, I came back from six weeks of short term study at Eastern Mennonite School wishing to take further course work but that was promptly squashed."

Although Pop was reared in a culture and a home that neither encouraged nor enabled higher education, reading and learning was deeply engrained in the fabric of their every day life. In fact, both Christian and Elsie Kurtz attended school past the eighth grade, which was above average for that era and that society. Dad's brother Paul writes: "Pop (Grandpa Kurtz) went through eight grades of school, repeating grade eight to broaden his vocabulary. He went four months to high school. Mom (Grandma Kurtz) started school early, got top grades, and finished two years of high school."

The tone set by the Kurtz Grandparents for their seven children included a value trilogy of hard work, dedicated service, and continual learning. Again, Paul Kurtz reflects, "Mom saw wisdom in the common things. She clipped and posted pictures and sayings around the home for us to observe and study. If we rushed into the house, climbing the stairs to hurry and get dressed to go back out, we ran past a prominent motto at every turn."

The family also had a radio, which afforded them the opportunity of keeping up with current events and news reports during the 1920s and 1930s and beyond. Dad remembers: "I recall the great speech I heard by radio from Winston Churchill."

Church speakers, pastors and missionaries visiting their local church also provided a window into a wider world for Dad and his siblings. Pop remembers in particular Pastor John S. Mast who made a very favorable impression upon him. "He visited our church and impressed me by the way he carried his posture, projected his voice, and delivered his sermons with great clarity, dignity, and helpful content."

For Pop there was even the educational opportunity of learning to speak a second language. "Scarlet fever was a feared disease in 1930," he writes. "Our hired man, Uncle Jake, was isolated with this dreaded disease so I was sent away for a month, for fear that I might catch this awful fever. I spent the month with Grandmother Stoltzfus and Aunt Emma Beiler. I learned the German language while there."

Each day during family altar time the children heard and/or read scriptures, sang hymns, and prayed prayers. Every week they memorized a Bible verse. There were also periodicals and books that the Kurtz children could read. As a young boy Dad recalls some of his most memorable books, including: "Pilgrim's Progress"; "The Prince of the House of David"; "Ben Hur"; "Papa Was a Preacher"; and, a children's series titled: "The Sugar Creek Gang."

Dad remembers a magazine regularly in their home that greatly influenced his theology and faith, "A high level magazine Papa had in the home was The Mennonite Quarterly Review. This scholarly periodical presented the thinking of students of Mennonite history, beliefs, and practices. Additionally, it included the oft-quoted essentials by writer and theologian Harold Bender in a section called 'The Anabaptist Vision.' This section included topics such as: brotherhood; love even of enemies; heavenly citizenship and primacy of scriptures."

This early and continual exposure to learning and reading provided Pop with a solid foundation to his later formal education. Going to school was motivational for Dad. He absorbed the lessons like a sponge. Again, it was for him a sense of privilege and blessing, for he was not assured how far he would be permitted to go in pursuit of his educational dreams. In fact, his level of commitment as a student did not go unnoticed by his high school peers who voted him the motto "The most earnest student." That very same motto would apply to Dad not only during his first year of high school, but throughout all of his years.

Dad spoke with fondness of his school teachers, especially a certain Mr. Alvin C. Aldefer, who taught him civics. Pop shares, "We followed Hitler's advance across Europe in that class. Mr. Aldefer did not keep to the text book but helped us discuss and follow current events."

As the eldest of five sons, Pop was groomed to eventually operate the family dairy farm. Therefore, formal education would not be as necessary. But, Dad heard a different call. And while he worked diligently on the family farm, he could never let go of his education vision.

Elam's son Kevin shares from his research: "Grandma Elsie perceived her son's interest in more education and suggested that Elam continue with a home-study program from the American School at Chicago."

So after elementary school and a portion of high school was concluded, Dad completed high school by taking a correspondence course in the early 1940s. He reflects: "When Lena (Dad's sister) planned to get her State Equivalent Diploma, and I provided her transportation, I registered for the same and got my G.E.D. likewise. With a Home Study Diploma and the Pennsylvania G.E.D., I matriculated at the Eastern Mennonite School for pre-medical courses."

As Kevin records, "At this time, Elam, now twenty-three years old, enrolled in college at Eastern Mennonite nearly two-hundred and fifty miles away from home in Harrisonburg, Virginia, but he kept a dairy farm seven extra months as an option to return."

Pursuing an educational dream at this level was a huge crossing and transition for Dad, given the expectations others had placed upon him as concerned his operating and managing the family's dairy farm. Yet the call to be a medical doctor was a calling he could not ignore. His sails were set. And, in 1947 Dad left farming for good. During the fall of 1947 he entered Eastern Mennonite College in Harrisonburg, Virginia. He spent one year in pre-medical education at EMC with an emphasis on studies in Biology. However, since the school was not yet academically approved by the accrediting associations he transferred. In 1948 he began studies at Lebanon Valley College. Believing that this was the proper path for his educational and vocational journey, Dad yielded the farm to his brother John, next in age. The crossing from farm to pursuit of another vocation had finally taken place.

At Lebanon Valley College Dad majored in Chemistry. Also while at LVC during his junior year he married his sweetheart, Orpah Horst, becoming simultaneously a committed husband and a dedicated student. Pop shares, "On our honeymoon I was so involved in my college courses at LVC that I took along my Organic Chemistry textbooks!"

Dad and Mom set up housekeeping in a mobile home, as Dad remembers: "We rented a twenty-eight foot trailer off of Lebanon Valley College campus, with a path to the outhouse. The view out of the kitchen window was Levi Miller's trailer, who also attended LVC. The view from our living room was a school building and tennis courts—where I took exercise from time to time."

Pop graduated with a Bachelor of Science degree in Chemistry from Lebanon Valley College in the spring of 1951. Upon graduation, Dad continued to pursue his doctoring dream. During the summer of 1951 he and Mom packed up and headed for Cleveland, Ohio, where Dad enrolled in medical school at Western Reserve University (now Case Western University). Reflecting upon his MD dream and his medical school experience, Pop writes: "It is like the metamorphosis that yields the butterfly or even like the fertilized egg that becomes a chick breaking the confining egg-shell. The resultant creature's self-realization is similar to the 'becoming' student's maturation into the 'real doctor.' Years of learning and case-reporting after collecting data and organizing the reporting transforms the nascent medical student into the practicing physician.

The motivations for becoming are so strong the student can be trusted to seek for self-realization. The raw materials are the patients newly entrusted to the would-be doctor who records the observations with the clinical impressions unfolding before the eager vision of a person's well-being enabled and enhanced."

Pop accomplished the educational crossing from nascent medical student to practicing physician, as he graduated with a medical degree from Western Reserve University in the spring of 1955. This was followed by a year of internship at St. Luke's Hospital in Shaker Heights, Ohio.

Upon completion of Dr. Kurtz's formal education the learning never ended for him. His life and years were filled with a pursuit of learning, application of that learning, and enabling others to learn. He attended seminars, conferences and workshops. He completed continuing education requirements through audio tapes for learning, correspondence courses and classes. In Pop's own words: "Family Practice includes forever learning from books and media, from colleagues, and even from the clients whom we serve."

Forever learning, continually growing, and voraciously reading, this was Elam Kurtz. Dad would often tell us children, "Books are your friends." Growing up he and Mom would often read to us, from books such as C.S.

Lewis' "The Lion, the Witch, and the Wardrobe" or, "Lucy Winchester" or, "A Book of Bible Stories." His daughter Karen recalls, "A book 'The Lady in the Green Hat' inspired Dad to load us up in the car and take us in search of an isolated Vermont village. There we located and met the first female auctioneer in the country."

At the age of seventy-six, Pop responded to the question, "What is your favorite way to spend a day of leisure"? He replied, "Reading, but I wish I didn't fall asleep so easily!"

Dad was well-read and widely read. His readings included medical journals, cultural and religious volumes, and world history writings. He could converse in an intelligent manner on diverse topics and themes.

His hunger to learn more about people and places led him to research and read. Very often, before and during our family travels Dad would purchase a book(s) about that very place or about a famous person who lived in that location. For example, during 2000, Dr. Kurtz, and his two sons Kevin and Michael travelled to the Holy Land. In preparation for this journey, Dad read the following books to better understand the land and the people of Israel: "Desire of the Everlasting Hills," "Israel," "Constantine the Great," "Herod," "The World of the Bible," "Israel: Past and Present," "The Geography of the Holy Land," and, "Battles of the Bible." This Holy Land bibliography sample is representative of the many times and ways in which Pop assimilated information and knowledge on a wide array of topics and subjects, so that he might be better informed and more educated on matters.

For Dad, it was as if life itself was a learning lab, filled with delightful discoveries and fascinating formulas. And, if persons were diligent and persistent in observing and learning, they would be certain to uncover mysteries and truths that could lead to deeper understandings and greater growth. But, even more rewarding, this growth in truth and understanding-- this learning--could be shared with others, thereby making their life more fulfilling and enriched.

Dad continued a lifetime of learning and growing until the day he left this earth. For him, life was not an existence to be tolerated, but, instead, a journey to be embraced and celebrated--a series of crossings to be enthusiastically navigated! His was a fluid life, as opposed to a frozen existence.

I believe that writer Gail Godwin's words in "The Finishing School" aptly and accurately describe Pop:

"There are two kinds of people......One kind, you can tell just by looking at them at what point they congealed into their final selves. It might be a....nice (enough) self, but you know you can expect no more

surprises from it. Whereas, the other kind, keep moving, changing.....
They are fluid. They keep moving forward and making new trysts with
life, and the motion of it keeps them young. In my opinion, they are the
only people who are still alive. You must be constantly on your guard.....
against congealing." (Viking Press, 1984; p.4).

Dad's quest for learning and zest for discovering kept him fluid.
This open stance to life and living enabled Pop to continually learn and
consistently grow.

CHAPTER THREE
VOCATIONAL CROSSINGS

"The key to the successful program are the preceptors. They must be teachers, counselors, and friends. They must want to learn as well as to teach." --Quotation from an unknown medical magazine.

Dr. Kurtz graduated from Western Reserve University School of Medicine on June 26th, 1955. On June 27th, Elam and Orpah Kurtz, along with their children Karen and Michael, loaded up their possessions and moved to Ashe County, North Carolina, where Dr. Kurtz would begin practicing medicine.

In his own words, "During the year of rotating internship, I received a call from an Ashe County Mennonite pastor, Aquilla Stoltzfus, sharing with me the great need for medical doctors and medical care in the mountains of North Carolina. I was then put in touch with the director of the Ashe Memorial Hospital, with whom I indicated my great interest in coming to Ashe County as a physician, and the rest was history.

Our second child, Michael David, was one year old to the day as we loaded up our 1950 Mercury and headed south. The ten-hour ride seemed to take forever, and particularly the final leg of the journey, as we encountered roads that included mountainous terrain and sharp curves, foreign to our driving experience. In fact, the winding mountain roads were so unfamiliar to us that they did not agree with Karen Joyce, our almost five-year-old, as she christened the town of Independence, Virginia with her stomach contents."

The crossing of the mountainous roads was, nonetheless, completed and the Kurtz Family set up house-keeping in Ashe County, which would become Dr. Kurtz's beloved home for nearly fifty-four years. The family started out in a small bungalow-style house that the Roland and Faw Builders had constructed in the town of Jefferson, at the request of Dr. Jones, Sr.

However, Dad, from the very beginning of this Ashe County "experiment" was uncertain as to how long, or even if, this newly formed doctor-Ashe County relationship would last. Dad was unsure how a northerner would be received in this southern culture. And, he was further not certain how a non-resistant, Mennonite stance would be perceived and accepted. As he expresses, "Did the medical community grant my entering the southland as a 'carpetbagger?' At least they expected me likely to be in North Carolina only briefly."

On the aforementioned peace position Dad relates, "One of my foundational principles for living and for serving as a physician was following the Christ-like non-violent, non-resistant stance. I also wished to serve my fellowman in non-violent activities. Faced with the likelihood of a doctor draft, I volunteered to do civilian service in work of national importance and in the field of choice--medicine. While an intern at St. Luke's Hospital in Shaker Heights, Ohio, a Dr. Nichols granted a weekend trip to visit a prospective site to practice medicine.

Dean C. Jones, Sr. considered my offer to come, even to serve Ashe County if my draft board gave the okay. Meanwhile, I met the recruiter for Ethiopia under the Eastern Mennonite Board of Missions and Charities. Should the door to Ashe County close, I would not be able to assist Dr. Jones, even though his work load was overwhelming. So, I made sure of a back up plan. There was some resistance to my being there. Dr. Jones had instructions to "Take any offer in preference of Elam Kurtz." So from November 1955 until June 1956 the future was uncertain. Dr. Jones had had some previous short-term assistance, so even the Medical Society expected another short-term servant in the back woods of North Carolina.

The Mennonite Central Committee provided Dr. Jones with the needed steps to undertake the employment of a conscientious objector. In addition, I found great support in Ashe County pastor Rev. Aquilla Stoltzfus, the person greatly responsible for my being in the mountains of North Carolina."

Thus, Dad began his medical practice in Ashe County by assisting Dean Cicero Jones, Sr. MD in his "overly busy practice with surgeries, medical cases, obstetrics, and community roles in abundance. He was understandably eager for a helper. He accepted my offer to help even though I was not supportive of the military. He was granted taking me on, but other offers were to be preferred. None came along, so I arrived sensing the need for more training beyond the year of rotating internship and beyond medical education at Western Reserve University."

On September 6, 1955, Dr. D. C. Jones, Sr. penned the following letter to Elam in Cleveland:

Dear Sir:

I have your card of inquiry concerning the hospital and the training program.

This is a fifty bed general hospital, located in the rural area, although it is at the County Seat of Ashe County. It is a non-profit hospital, operated by a Board of Directors, and I am the Superintendent, Medical Director and Chief Surgeon.

We do not have a formal training program, and are not qualified to give training of interns or residents for credit with any boards. Neither do we have nurse's training.

However, we do keep a full time physician here as assistant to me, at all times when a suitable one is available. While he gets no formal course of training, and cannot get resident credit for boards, the ones I have had have generally gotten in the accredited residencies. It is actually experience under my observation and freely given consultation any time desired or needed by the assistant.

The work consists of general medical and surgical care, obstetrics and much emergency care of acute illnesses and injuries. It is both with in-patients and out-patients, and does furnish a good introduction to general practice.

We pay what I think is a rather good salary for a young man starting out. The last man we had has just left, going into psychiatric residency. The position is therefore open.

In case you should be interested in this position, please write me, and send some particulars of your self, family responsibilities and your training. Also please send a few references from staff physicians or hospital officials where you are now working.

Sincerely yours,
D. C. Jones, M.D.

Dad goes on to explain, "In my own development, I was fortunate to have a practice mentor in Ashe County in the person of Dr. Jones, Sr., who was available to me right after internship, as I was not yet quite prepared to go health-care alone. With good texts and his standing by I perceived the learning curve continuing a vigorous advancement. I advanced to a see-one-do-one mentality, so that in the mentor's absence I could perform successfully treating fractures, breech deliveries, gastric ruptures and acute appendicitis cases."

It was readily apparent that Dr. Jones needed assistance with patient case loads. It was also obvious that Dr. Jones and Dad made a great team in their mentor-mentee relationship, and Dad's presence made it possible for Doc Jones to pursue some much-needed away from the practice time. Dad remembers, "Dr. Jones and his wife, Lettie, and their son Dean Jones, Jr., had only two rooms and a bath from which 'Dean' would be on call almost continually, if not fishing. Most morning hours consisted of surgery cases, then lunch and reading to prepare for the next day's procedures. This was followed in the afternoon and evening hours with office visits for twenty to thirty out-patients. Dr. Jones did 'rounds' on in-patients in forenoons and evenings, as required.

The first week that I took duty for the hospital, the local high school principal and Dean couldn't safely exit the Long Hope area after fishing, due to weather conditions and darkness, so Mrs. Jones and I waited up almost all night fearing a patient-child's elbow fracture could eventuate into a Volkmann's contracture. So before daylight we sent him to the nearest medical center at Baptist Hospital in Winston-Salem, NC, by funeral home 'ambulance.' I must have done an adequate job in Dr. Jones' absence because following this episode he was willing to delegate to me as his back-up. When he was not available and urgent cases presented, I undertook cases such as breech obstetrical deliveries and in the surgical area closed perforated gastric ulcers and performed a few appendectomies."

The position at Ashe Memorial Hospital, the teamwork with Dr. Jones, and the relocation to Ashe County were all a wonderful fit for Dad. All the questions and doubts that seemed so prevalent early on while transitioning now dissipated. A letter from Dad, addressed to his parents on January 20th, 1957 speaks to this positive chemistry.

> Dear Papa and Mama,
>
> On this anniversary weekend, greetings!
>
> We are enjoying the visit of Papa and Mama Horst.
>
> Thank you for the hospitality when we come your way.
>
> It is, however, good to be at home again and back at the work I'd rather do than any thing else.

It is still leaving me wondering how it can possibly be that we are so privileged to assist at this fine hospital, under such a fine associate, and among such wonderful people as these of Ashe County. For your part in directing us this way we thank you.

Elam

During the year prior to Dr. Kurtz arriving to work with Dr. Jones Sr. in Ashe County, Dr. W.J. Robinson, who practiced medicine in the Creston area, passed away. This made the already critical shortage of doctors in Ashe County and surrounding areas even more of a crisis. In addition to working in Jefferson with Dr. Jones at Ashe Memorial Hospital, Dr. Kurtz also worked one evening a week at the office where Dr. Robinson had practiced.

Dr. Joseph Robinson married an Ashe County girl, Julie Sutherland of Sutherland, N.C., who persuaded her new physician-husband to practice medicine in Ashe County. Years earlier, while vacationing in Ashe County, Doc acquired such a great love for the place that he decided to settle there. Then he opened up an office in Creston at his home. His hours were anytime day or night seven days a week. He would even make house calls in the community as needed. If someone was sick and did not have the money to pay, he treated them anyway.

Doc traveled around Ashe County on horseback, providing medical assistance to anyone who needed it. He helped people by delivering babies, setting bones, and even pulling teeth. The job was a difficult one, because modern equipment as we know it was unheard of in those days. Doc purchased his medical supplies from S.E. Medical of Bristol, Tennessee.

He delivered his first baby when he was eighteen years old. Since this writing is focusing upon crossings, it seems appropriate that the following Dr. Robinson story be included. Once when a creek had overflowed its banks, Dr. Robinson, undaunted by the elements, swam his horse across it to deliver a baby whose family resided on the other side.

Dr. Robinson was graciously received and greatly loved by the people of Ashe County whom he faithfully served for fifty years. Doc Robinson also left big shoes to fill. Dr. Kurtz made an effort to help fill that missing medical doctor void. As he records, "One month after Dr. Robinson's death I had been invited to help Ashe County fill that medical care position by a Mennonite pastor at the Big Laurel Mennonite Church. Upon arriving in June of 1956, and continuing for two years, while practicing under Dean C. Jones, Sr. MD, I went to the Robinson office on Monday nights and acquired patients that remained with me until retirement in 2003."

Like Dr. Robinson before him, Dr. Kurtz also was both sensitive and attentive to the medical needs of Ashe County's citizens. He served these folk with the best he could give. This included many house calls, sometimes in the middle of the night. As a young boy, I recall going on several house calls with my Dad. While Dad could do some rudimentary examinations in persons' homes, and while he had a few medical instruments in his doctor's black bag, what probably helped more than anything was a physician who cared enough to check in with them as patients, listen to them, and give some words of encouragement, such as, "Get some rest. I know you'll get better. And, I'll check back with you soon."

I remember several times traveling on house calls with Dad, driving deep into some mountain hollows, even a couple times fording creeks in our black VW Bug to get to his patients' homes. There was even an occasion when one of Dr. Kurtz's medical students made a house call by crossing the New River on a pole boat. During the early 1970s Duke student Margaret Higham was assisted across the river to Roscoe Neaves' residence to attend to his invalid wife, Winnie. Margaret carried Dr. Kurtz's black Knickerbocker doctor bag that when fully loaded with I V fluids weighed over 40 pounds.

Sometimes patients would pay a nominal house call fee. But there were also occasions when we would receive a stack of wood at our home, or a sugar-cured ham, or some other item that appreciative patients brought to Pop, sometimes as "bartering" payment for his medical services for they did not have the financial means to pay for his services. Dad was always okay with this, as he cared far more about their health than about financial gain.

While Dad provided the old-fashioned house calls to his patients who could not come to him, he at the same time sought to provide quality care with state of the art medical equipment and services at a clinic he established.

In 1958 Dr. Kurtz began this clinical solo practice in Lansing, N.C., thereby serving the people of the northwestern portion of Ashe County as well as many patients from southwest Virginia. Dad brought affordable, excellent quality healthcare to this rural, more isolated area. Through the years, Dr. Kurtz established an office which offered among other services, X-ray capabilities, medical laboratory services, as well as a small in-house pharmacy. A staff, as large as ten persons at one time, enabled a lot of medical services to be dispensed to many folk during each office work day.

Describing the Lansing clinic, Dr. Kurtz writes: "Within my solo practice I had a receptionist-office organizer with Mrs. Kurtz also helping in this area and I dictated notes in the next office room. Across the entry hall was the dispensary providing the ordered new medications for physician review and for educational literature, often a practice-generated document. Next was the laboratory and beyond that an x-ray room that could also serve as an emergency room. Directly behind the physician's dictating room was located the stenographer who was also patient-accessible and often a confidante. In the community she became an extension of the practice, often helping a questioning client. Beside her room was a small pediatric room with scales to weigh children and space for the autoclave. Clockwise were three rooms for the patients, in which there were office assistants with these duties: data gathering, treatment plan, sometimes educational films previously ordered or procedures scheduled, specific education, and assisting the physician's examination. These staff persons were trained to provide full preparation for patient needs, with patient instructions and treatment goals and schedules, if applicable. The same office assistant carried out tests and/or treatments with explanations and outlined strategies. The office visit was completed with front-office discussion of plans and costs and other unanswered questions. There was also a large waiting area where contagious cases had privacy.

Such a complex approach to give detailed attention to efficiency and comprehensive care was a major task for the team to satisfactorily explain, and sometimes even justify, but the 'sales-resistance' was overcome in time. With the aid of an entry questionnaire new patients were amazed at the patient-knowledge a practitioner could gather with the time and help of the office assistants. In addition, the stenographer could, and did, send appropriate notes to case-consultants, obtain needed reports from medical resources, and compose letters of referral and follow-up."

There was time and space in the Lansing clinic for other helpers: psychology interns, a psychologist, and for two years a NIMH-granted psychiatrist, who attended part-day weekly. Dr. Kurtz reflects, "With an available on call psychiatrist I had the same desired association in my own practice for the most cared for and motivated clients. Here I found what I believed was all along the front-line for mental health care. I considered this integrative care to be the most efficient, most cost-effective, and most satisfying model for both patient and physician."

As mentioned in an earlier chapter, Dr. Kurtz was interested in and committed to the practice of holistic medicine. Therefore, the integration of good physical health care with good mental health care made perfectly good sense to Kurtz. Further fostering this integration of disciplines, another educational, holistic care opportunity came to Ashe County when James Cathell, a retired mental hospital administrator envisioned a

National Institute of Mental Health grant to serve rural North Carolina. Dr. Cathell anticipated only a few practitioners might find his consultations acceptable or even useful. On this topic Dr. Kurtz shares, "I had detoured from my first notion to train in the mental health field because I did not care for the psychiatric models in school or internship. I saw the need could be met by family practice, even general practice at that time. Dr. Cathell was delighted to find many primary care physicians utilized his services. For a while, after two years' instruction on my own clients, I considered psychological medicine as my subspecialty. A few years later, Family Medicine embraced this cause and encouraged these physicians to provide more total care including addressing psychological needs."

Dad had an intense awareness of the importance of and need for good mental health care. And he became a strong advocate of providing this mental health care both inside his practice and outside the clinic. Mental health advocacy and education became one of his passions. As is often the case, areas of great focus and passion are often driven by personal experiences, sometimes painful experiences.

Dad reflects, "The goals for my medical training were the prevention of, and relief of, mental illness. It had destroyed a promising and planned-for-marriage in my own life. A young lady to whom I was engaged suffered from the symptoms and negative effects of mental illness. Her relatives and community members who had themselves suffered their share from her symptomatic behaviors advised that the engagement be broken. The advice was heeded and the engagement was ended. From this painful experience I chose to better understand and serve such afflicted persons."

Yet another personal history piece that influenced Dad, in his earlier years, to show great empathy with those struggling from the effects of mental illness was the compassion he witnessed of his parents for the mentally ill. Dad remembers, "Papa and Mama were very supportive of the patients at Wernersville Mental Hospital west of Reading, PA. They lamented the depersonalization of the treatments, the lack of psychiatric rehabilitation, and the evident lack of empathy toward the patients. From their testimony I became interested in mental health issues.

I intensely absorbed skills and information in appropriate treatments, referrals, and enhanced leadership in community mental health. Dr. Cathell favored my office with once a month visits. On the evenings of that day he and I spent time reviewing cases that had accumulated, while seated in the dining area of the Colvard Manor, where he chose to stay while in Ashe County. Dr. Cathell readily understood the skills and aptitudes of the 'student-doctors' he tutored."

In the November 1968 issue of "Today's Health" published by The

American Medical Association, columnist Mike Michaelson wrote an article titled "Psychiatry Comes to the Grass Roots," in which Dr. Cathell's consultation with Dr. Kurtz is noted: "'The Family,' says Doctor Cathell, 'is a key person in the treatment of emotional illness. He has an intimate knowledge of his patients and their histories, and, often, the histories of their families--and has a good rapport with them. His presence during births, deaths, and other crises promotes close, personal relationships--often through several generations, and puts him in a unique position to recognize developing psychiatric disorders and to act on them before they become bigger and more serious.'

One man who 'really wanted to see' the consultant is Elam S. Kurtz, M.D, a general practitioner and the only physician in the charming Blue Ridge Mountain community of Lansing. An intense, ascetic man of the Mennonite faith, Doctor Kurtz maintains that 'physicians in General Practice are at the forefront of psychiatry, and in the battle against mental illness the psychiatrist becomes a very important ally. I think we readily could utilize the consultant's visits twice a month,' he adds.

'Every patient, even though his illness may be organic, has a component of psychological need,' says Doctor Kurtz. 'The availability of a psychiatric consultant can help the general practitioner meet that need. Given the effective tools of psychiatric management, the community physician will find that the uninteresting case becomes interesting, the bothersome patient becomes a challenge.'

Endorsing the important role of community agencies in mental-health care, Doctor Kurtz relates that the local welfare agency frequently will refer patients to him, indicating that there may exist psychiatric disturbances with which he might help. 'I also have developed a good working relationship with ministers,' says Doctor Kurtz, 'who often will drop by the office to discuss parishioners. They provide useful follow-up support, which frequently results in fewer office visits.'"

NIMH perceived the consultative benefit to the local physicians and continued the supportive resource for another two years, following Dr. Cathell, with Brooke Johnson, a behavioral psychologist, who continued to provide excellent consultation and support.

Dr. Kurtz became more and more involved in mental health causes and advocacy, "When the North Carolina Department of Human Resources accepted the challenge of human rights, I got repeated invitations to take part. The volunteers visited in-patients and advocated for them and the staff. We were encouraged to find out if the patients had a plan of treatment and if they either knew of it or were aware thereof. Sadly, even the most alert and intelligent did not have knowledge of this information."

Dad's volunteer work with The New River Mental Health received a lot of his energy and time, "Ashe County had for a number of years an active chapter in Mental Health. I was appointed a regional Vice President for our state and participated in a number of center-site visits on behalf of the state volunteer organization. Most interesting to me was the director at Culhowhee, NC, who with similar organizational style and skills to mine had doubled his county's mental health budget all five years since the center's inception and was able to involve ex-patients. This positive example inspired me to advocate even more for mental health needs. For almost thirty years I attended as a member of our Mental Health Board."

As passionate as Dad was about being a mental health advocate, there was probably one vocationally-related aspect about which he was even more passionate. That was the mentoring of medical students! Dad loved to teach. And, he loved to mentor. And when he could teach and mentor centering upon his passion of medicine and the application of this discipline as manifest in the patient-physician relationship, he was in his element. With the teaching and mentoring of medical students, Dad had truly found his vocational niche, for this integrated his love and gifts of teaching, mentoring, and medicine simultaneously!

From the late 1960s until the early 1990s Dr. Kurtz was continually and intensely involved in mentoring medical students. In fact, there were a total of fifty-six students in a span of some twenty-five years! And, an enormous blessing for Dad was that his fifty-sixth, and final, medical student was his own son, Kevin.

Dr. Kurtz's passion and enthusiasm is expressed in his own words, "To teach medical students is a great joy. They, in turn, enjoy teaching other eager students. I plan to keep medical students in Ashe County year round." Dad had learned and embraced the concept of being a teacher of teachers of teachers. Not just teaching. Not just teaching other teachers (medical students); but, teaching medical students who would then teach others. This was exponential growth and a ripple of influence. This was the proven route to having the maximum positive influence upon the maximum number of persons!

For this style of learning to be both authentic and effective called for vulnerability and openness demonstrated by the mentor before the mentee. It called for a two-way learning context. Not only would the mentee learn from the mentor, but in this open, two-way process, the mentor was also certain to learn and grow. On this two-way learning style, Dr. Kurtz observes, "Not all the learning was from the preceptor since the student contributed also. For example, my first clinically-oriented student had just had an off-site rotation in Dermatology. From this experience he taught me to biopsy difficult skin lesions." Or, again, on this two-way approach to learning, Dad writes, "Learning alongside students was both challenging and exciting for me and my office staff." Later, in a published article which he wrote, Dr. Kurtz readily admits, "Recently I had a chance to communicate with a medical student on the practice of medicine--but what a switch from the usual procedure! I learned from the student how to do it!"

One of the motivating reasons for Dr. Kurtz mentoring students and for stressing the need for two-way and hands-on learning in the physician-student relationship was the fact that his medical school experience did not provide that practical method of learning which he so desired. Reflecting on this topic, Dad writes, "At the school of medicine I attended, in the third year it was deemed wise to expose students to doctors in practice. I was assigned an internist whose specialty often serves complicated cases.

I waited patiently for the doctor to teach me, an eager learner. No patient was seen or discussed. No pretend case came for discussion, no chief complaint or known history or lab data--only a tube of blood with its 'sed (sedimentation) rate' came my way, which meant the blood cells stayed where they began if normal but dropped to indicate possible disease.

The internist then should have explained the rationale for the test and the next steps to be taken, with both the patient and me, the medical student. At that doctor-patient visit I did not perceive a positive, inquiring relationship modeled, as neither informed consent for examination nor treatment plans or follow-up strategies were presented to the client.

The internist missed opportunities to inform and challenge a student who wanted to observe teaching. When my first clinical student initiated his own 'hands-on' involvement, I thoroughly agreed and maintained that same interactive teaching relationship and posture with fifty-six grateful participants."

During the 1960s and 1970s rural areas in the United States faced an extreme shortage of doctors. In an effort to help remedy this, the North Carolina Medical Society issued a plea to practicing physicians. Dad received a letter dated August 8, 1972 from NCMS in which the opening paragraphs read, "Rural North Carolina faces a crying need for more physicians. With these cries in mind in our State and other areas of the country, the Student American Medical Association is sponsoring an effort to lure more medical students to practice in rural areas within their state.

Pre-clinical medical students from Bowman Gray, Duke University and the University of North Carolina will be matched with sponsors for an 8-10 week period during the summer season. The students will be exposed to the medical services, doctors' offices, and community health facilities. We urge and encourage you to consider hosting a student for the summer."

Responding with swiftness and enthusiasm to this invitation to mentor students, Dad sought certification from all three of the afore-mentioned institutions, of which he was granted acceptance. One such letter of certification, sent from The University of North Carolina at Chapel Hill granting Dr. Kurtz Clinical Instructor status, stated:

> Dear Dr. Kurtz:
> I want to advise you that your appointment as Clinical Instructor in the Department of Family Medicine, School of Medicine, has been approved by the Vice Chancellor for Health Affairs. I wish to thank you for your contributions to the Department and to the School.
>
> Sincerely,
> Stuart Bondurant, M.D.

Dad worked intentionally at being the very best preceptor he could be to his students. He wanted them to have as medical students what he as a medical student longed for but did not have. Located in Dr. Kurtz's files was a brief article that he had identified as "essential" for a positive doctor-student relationship. It is entitled, "What Is a Preceptor":

"A good preceptor should accomplish the following things: 1. He should help the medical students learn about general practice by letting him observe (most patients will not object if the student's status is explained) and by discussing the case and its implications later. 2. Help the student to understand the rationale of treating colds, headaches, back aches, and other common minor ailments. 3. As mutual confidence and trust is established between the preceptor and preceptee, let the student diagnose and give his proposed treatment of a given case. 4. Help the student to become familiar with methods in greeting patients, of questioning them, of listening to them, of examining them and of discussing fees with them. 5. Address the student as "doctor," it helps his self-confidence considerably. 6. Invite the student to offer opinions and to overcome his natural fear of being wrong. Accepting him as a near doctor creates a supportive atmosphere and will encourage his making a diagnosis or promoting an opinion. Encourage a student to accompany the doctor on follow up house calls and on follow up examinations of the patients in the hospital. 7. Permit the student to accept some responsibility. Most of them will do it well. Frequently the student can make afternoon or evening hospital rounds, by himself or separately. Encourage him to attend all night emergency cases, check on intravenous procedures, and allow him to suture minor lacerations under supervision. 8. Discuss with the student the cost of entering practices and the methods of financing the practice. Students are naturally interested in such matters and they need guidance, as well, concerning fees and other administrative items."

Dr. Kurtz worked at, and studied about, being the best mentor he could be. He read, reflected, practiced, and even wrote about this calling and passion of mentoring. Some of his writings were published and circulated nationally, such as his article "The Student Preceptorship Program: A Personal Experience," which appeared in the September 1970 issue of "The North Carolina Medical Journal."

The following excerpts are taken from this article on the preceptorship program, "I am convinced that medical students seldom learn the kind of medicine that is needed by mankind. The goals of training are geared to upper and middle-class pursuits of health.

A new generation of physicians is emerging, one inspired more by altruism than gain, preparing not to serve science but to relate science to man. Today's student of medicine welcomes the challenge of the family practice of medicine; but he must be exposed to it, for only then can rural needs become attractive to him....."

Dad received numerous requests for copies of the above-mentioned article to copy and distribute, which he readily and willingly granted each request. Once again, Dad was teaching teachers of teachers in an exponential manner as he reflected upon and placed in writing his experiences and observations.

For twenty-five years Dr. Kurtz placed working with and training medical students very high on his vocational priority list. He maintained his preceptor status with the three aforementioned medical schools and continually welcomed students into his Lansing practice in Ashe County. One of his former medical students wrote the following which appeared as the heading on a medical school profile page, describing the Ashe County experience with Dr. Kurtz:

"A very rewarding eight weeks with an energetic, academically geared family practitioner whose ability to evaluate the organic and functional needs of his patients is unexcelled. The location of the externship is ideal for relaxation, recreation and many cultural opportunities. This has been by far the most rewarding eight weeks I have spent in my two

years in medical school. I would encourage any student with interest in family practice to spend at least eight weeks in a similar environment; or, if fortunate enough, with Dr. Kurtz."

The remainder of this profile page provided demographic and community statistics concerning the student appointment. For example, students were informed that Ashe County was a rural mountain county with a population of some 20,000. The medical students could expect sixty hours and up per week in practice. Weekly outpatient visits average 150 with an additional 15 to 20 in-patients at the local hospital per week. The percentage of time spent at the Lansing office equaled 80% of their time. With the remaining 20% divided between hospital and community time. Degree of latitude for students: First-year students may be community-based to observe health needs and resources of Ashe County, and/or they may serve as first assistant doing history taking, procedures, and assist in examination.

Subsequent years, students may be ready for clinical duties under supervision involving all or part of the following: Screening office patients; Screening emergency room patients; and, History-physical and summaries and evening rounds at local hospital.

As the word got out about the receptivity and gracious hospitality offered medical students by Dr. and Mrs. Kurtz, the office staff, and, indeed, the people of Ashe County, applications steadily arrived. During their 8 to 10 week internship students were housed in a variety of ways. Some stayed in local motels. Others stayed with the Kurtz family. Later, students were housed in a home in Lansing, acquired for this very purpose and located within walking distance of the clinic.

While the medical practice was demanding of both energy and time, there was always time for recreation and relaxation in the beautiful Ashe County Mountains, and surrounding areas. Leisure and off time activities included among others: Mountain climbing, bike riding, trips to Abingdon, Virginia's Barter Theatre, church meetings, snow skiing, and the frequently offered invitation of playing chess with Dr. Kurtz.

Relationships developed and friendships grew as students became woven into the fabric of the life of a small, rural mountain county. A written representative (there were many more students) list of medical students assisting under Dr. Kurtz's supervision reads:

"My first clinical student was from Winston-Salem, Bowman Gray School of Medicine, who elected and was granted a rotation. He had previously participated in a Duke rotation in Dermatology.

From this Duke experience Bill taught me something that served me well through the years when faced with a dermatological dilemma: 'If you don't perceive the diagnosis from appearance, then biopsy.' Mr. Tucker became a cardiac surgeon and, in fact, was on stand by, when Dr. Kutcher was performing my own angioplasty for a nearly occluded LAD, that held for seventeen years before a quadruple bypass was necessary."

Dad recalls what was to be the final Ashe County funeral home "ambulance ride", on which medical student Bill Tucker participated:

"Bill Tucker, my first medical student, assisted on the emergency transportation of a twelve-year-old with stiff-lung disorder from presumed insecticide exposure. Bill assisted in bag-breathing en route from Jefferson, N.C., from the Ashe Memorial Hospital to the North Carolina Baptist Hospital in Winston-Salem.

Reins-Sturdivant Funeral Home provided the vehicle and Jim Hartley was the careful driver, avoiding an unpredictable cow on Route 163 near the cemetery made famous by a Daniel Boone relative's interment.

Our patient was given first-rate care under cardiologist-neurologist, Dr. James O'Toole, who determined after the patient expired that the stiff lung arose from the central nervous system's inflammatory reaction of an auto-immune origin.

This was the final time the funeral homes' vehicles served a dual duty as concerned these transportation topics. As some Ashe County citizen quipped, that might have been a 'conflict of interest!'"

Another of Dr. Kurtz's students published some of her Ashe County medical student experiences. Carol Weed, from California and Woman's Medical College in Philadelphia, was encouraged by the Health Department to study the health delivery system in Ashe County. She was impressed by the nearly magical power the primary care physician displayed.

Following are summary comments from Carol Weed upon completion of her 10-week experience in Ashe County:

Commendable About Appalachia

- "I had a ball! I learned things not taught in a medical school. Many earthly needs are met by Appalachians without cash. Physical accessibility to health care exists.

- I had many opportunities to discuss issues with a number of persons in and out of the health fields. The Southern hospitality was fantastic. I found refreshing exposure to the value and time system of the mountain folk. It was less frustrating than city contacts. I found a little more time to meet people, talk with people, and do more together. I also found a particular patience in mountain folk, and their willingness to listen. This results in a value of persons over things.
- I felt I made a positive contribution during this experience and that my ideas were listened to and at least considered."

Among The New Things Learned

- "I learned so much about the practice of a general practitioner. I also learned about the varieties of barriers to health care and the prevalence of accidents in rural areas. Further, I gained insight through this experience concerning the business aspects of medicine; the efficient operation of a practice; the values of a fee for service; and, the amazing endurance of body and soul."

Reinforced

- "Confirmed for me through this 10-week term were the following:
  o The value of health education and preventive medicine.
  o The value of practical, applied psychiatry.
  o The value of a potential for increased paramedical personnel.
  o The significance of priorities in problem-solving.
  o The richness of Appalachia not measured in dollars and sense."

Things Not Commendable

- "Observations that were not commendable during my service in Appalachia:
  - Three barriers to health care in descending order of importance: Attitudes; Insufficient number of Doctors; and Financial Considerations.
  - Health professionals are overworked and inefficient use of medical and dental resources.
  - Lack of enough health care communications: Schools, T.V., Radio, Clinics, Community meetings.
  - Lack of vision for preventive care among low income people.
  - Too much red tape required to provide publically funded care.
  - The lack of established agencies to see those needing health care resources."

SUGGESTIONS

- "Here are some suggestions I propose:
  - Education for understanding health care resources.
  - Increased use of paramedical personnel.
  - Training patients and families for more self care.
  - Consider other sources of funding such as pre-paid plans.
  - Insurance should include preventive services as a means of decreasing health care costs.
  - Fees: A sliding scale is important no matter what system is used.
  - Hire doctors to do emergency room work."

* *

"John Lawrence was the first Duke student. He taught me how to listen to patients, and even personnel, to a level of concern I had never previously experienced. Kendra Lewis was the second student from Duke. Her strengths included enabling person-to-person relationships with regional practitioners.

'Buster' Farrington opened the way here for UNC-Chapel Hill students. Farrington is currently in practice with another of my students who experienced the same rural rotation, 'Bucky' Robert McNeill, a native of Ashe County.

Paul Grant was one of three or four of my students who were granted a return experience. He was later invited to serve the office and local hospital in locum tenens briefly.

My son, Kevin Kurtz, my 56th and final student, and Leigh Bradley met in Family Practice residencies in Asheville, NC, from which each was granted an office rotation. When they began a group practice in Ashe County they kindly invited my participation."

Dad continued to engage, educate, and learn from the many students he tutored. His underlying motive and foundational purpose was to enable these students to make the successful crossing from eager student to competent physician so that persons might be recipients of the highest quality health-care. In Dad's own words, "It became my pleasure to behold youthful and eager scholars undertaking health-care duties and thus 'crossing over' into the medical field!"

The time, commitment, and high priority that Dr. Kurtz gave to this student enterprise was acknowledged and deeply appreciated by his interns. The following are just a few excerpts from letters of gratitude addressed to Dr. Kurtz by his students.

"Dr. Kurtz, My eight weeks in Lansing was a very happy as well as profound experience for me. Even though we discussed it many times, I want to say again what a thrill it is to finally make some moves on my own, to finally do that thing which has been so long desired. I am particularly grateful for the chance to have that experience in a distinctly Christ-oriented setting, since it was He who started me on this path four years ago. Thank you for making all that possible."

"Dr. Kurtz, Thank you for the very helpful preceptorship. The key items in the preceptorship for me were to see the variants of normality and the immediate feedback with office visits. I was impressed that your patients had a lot of confidence in you as a physician and felt that you were a good friend as well. My next month will be spent in the classroom during the morning and in the Family Clinic during the afternoon. This staff will have a tough act to follow."

"Dear Dr. Kurtz, I want to thank you, your wife, and children for making my stay in Jefferson and Lansing very enjoyable and beneficial. I appreciated very much the interest and attention which you and your

family have shown to me. The medical experience and education which I received will prove tremendously valuable in my future."

"Dear Dr. Kurtz and Family, I've been looking back at my experience in Ashe County with much fondness. I shall long remember encounters made with the likes of Joe Gilley, Georgia Seagle, and Geneva Roark. It was all there, the triumph and the tragedy alike, and I appreciated being a part of it all. I think I have a better understanding now of the role that the family physician should fulfill as healer, comforter and counselor to his patients, by the example I have seen in your practice.

I want to thank all of you at the office who help the good doctor, for the enthusiasm with which you do your work, and the helpful hand you give the students. You make the 'team concept' really work.

Finally, I would like to thank you and your family for welcoming me into your Christian worship and fellowship at Meadowview. I admired the sense of community of your small groups, and enjoyed sharing some of that with you. I feel that I grew spiritually as well as intellectually during this elective because of your influence."

Last, but certainly not least, concerning Dr. Kurtz's vocational crossings, in 1972 he made the transition from General Practitioner to Family Practitioner. At this point in medical history General Practice Medicine, in many ways, seemed to have run its course. GP's had lost clout in the medical community. Kurtz reflects, "The general practice of medicine has been overshadowed by specialization with no captain of the team, one who can become the entry point and follow-up of the health-care resources. The choice to become an accredited Family Practitioner was very important to Dad. As he expresses, "The decision to cross from the field of General Practice to that of Family Practice was of extreme importance to me, as well as the field of medicine itself. No longer would the generalist be labeled disparagingly an 'LMD'. The American Medical Association saw wisdom in providing a specialty status for those qualifying. The new specialty included family practice residents, generalists who passed board examination, and grandfathered in those whose post-graduate efforts met the standards of the American Academy of Family Practice (AAFP). Medical schools, then, sought qualified teachers for students to see and experience first-hand the local clinic under the supervision of a Family Practitioner. I was fortunate to be a member of the largest entering class that met in New York City in 1972, where the keynote speaker was Senator Edward Kennedy."

Dad admired and appreciated Senator Kennedy's support of, and advocacy for, the Family Practice specialty. In later years this "Kennedy connection" was deepened, as Dr. Kurtz's daughter Becky was a classmate with Edward's niece, Caroline Kennedy, at Columbia Law School.

Dr. Kurtz continues on the topic of Family Practice certification, "Upon certification, medical schools awarded faculty status to those of us who elected to supervise and teach new students."

This new specialty accreditation coupled with the teaching opportunities it offered, gave renewed energy and motivation to Dad and to his practice of medicine. The practice of medicine combined with the teaching of students fit so well for him. It was his vocational passion. It was his calling. He had found his "sweet spot." Now his God-given gifts were being utilized and applied as never before.

Expressing his delight in making this crossing, Dad shared: "I wish to promote the role of the Family Practitioner for American medicine. I find it the most economical, most efficient, and the most needed in our hurting society. Family Practice offers a community health program what it needs most. If there are no mental health resources, no psychiatric skills, no Pediatric or Obstetrical professionals, no Surgical or Orthopedic talents, or no pulmonary and rehabilitative services, the all-inclusive Family Practice field can readily create a resource upon which a health-services institution can tailor its goals. I am glad I made this crossing!"

For Dad, being a physician was far more than a profession or a career. It was a divine calling. From leaving the family dairy farm to going to college and later medical school, it was a calling. From going from Case Western University to Ashe County, NC to work with Dr. Dean C. Jones, Sr. and then on to solo practice in Lansing and finishing as one of the practitioners in a group practice with his son, it was a calling. From examining patients to teaching students it was a calling. Going from General Practitioner to Family Practitioner, it was a calling.

It was a calling Dr. Kurtz loved and a calling he performed with persistence and with excellence. And, it was a calling by which he was humbled, and for which he was extremely grateful.

I close this chapter on vocational crossings with Dad's expressions of thankfulness and gratitude for the vocational calling: "Now that I have enjoyed the Family Practice career and see its potential for comprehensive and continuing patient service, I wish to thank those who made the opportunity available for me and those who were my teachers while in active practice: the medical schools who gave me faculty status; the Family Practice AMA advancement; the local hospital whose staff complemented these 'hatching' efforts. Perhaps this testimony can spark and encourage the interest and support for primary care which I perceive as the most rewarding, most challenging and the most cost-effective model available.

I offer my practice as an example and a promising experiment in medical education for the patients, for the students, and even for the supervising doctor. My students have honored me with their trust, their participation, and their encouragement. I am both honored and humbled by this joyous journey. To all involved along the way I say 'Thank you' and 'Shalom.'

Dr. C. D. Esch: Dr. Kurtz's relative and mentor

Road in Creston named for Dr. Robinson

Dr. Kurtz's Lansing, NC office

Crossing the New River--House call by Pole Boat

Dr. Elam S. Kurtz, MD

CHAPTER FOUR
RELATIONAL CROSSINGS

Dad was born April 1ˢᵗ, 1924 to Elsie and Christian Kurtz in the Conestoga Valley of Pennsylvania. His mother recounted that Dr. Mengel, who delivered Dad, told her, "He's the ugliest baby I ever saw!"

Pop was the oldest of seven siblings, five boys and two girls. He was named for his Amish maternal grandfather, Elam Stoltzfus, who died at age twenty-six of "galloping consumption." Dad reflects, "Evidently my family was well instructed in preventive methods, for in spite of a history suggesting TB, I entered medical school with a negative tuberculin test."

Elam was blessed to be raised by Christian parents in a supportive family. He came from a long line of love. That family line and lineage is contained at the conclusion of this chapter in the Elam Kurtz family genogram. A genogram is a genealogical map, placing several generations of a family in a concise diagram. Birth dates, dates of death, and other information is provided on family members. Genograms are informative resources and therapeutic tools to help persons learn more about their family of origin and thereby learning more about one self.

Pop's family was large in number, German-Swiss in background, and Mennonite by denomination. There appears to be no divorce on the family tree. There was one known case of alcoholism, that being Dad's paternal grandfather, Jacob Kurtz. As a result of this problem Jacob left his family and the farm and abdicated these responsibilities to his wife Lydia. Lydia became a very strong and self-sufficient woman, as the situation demanded. Fortunately, there were relatives who did help with the farm work. Yet, life was very tough for this family and the fierce independence and the somberness that resulted left an influence upon succeeding generations-- both positive and negative.

In spite of the dysfunction, disease, and eventual desertion of the family by Elam's grandfather Jacob, his father, Christian, through the guidance and support of his mother, Lydia, and a supportive extended family, found himself on a positive path. In 1922 he married Elsie Stoltzfus and the two commenced housekeeping and farming in Pennsylvania's Conestoga Valley.

Commenting on his father, Pop shares, "He was a farmer-preacher and was diligently occupied with both callings. I greatly admired his interest in publications and writings. He consistently sought to learn and grow. Because of his example I sought involvement in agricultural pursuits, even though they did not turn out to be my chosen path.

Growing up, I experienced Papa as a kind but stern gentleman, with good goals for living. He would always say to us, 'Don't forget who you are.'

I did perceive a dogmatic approach in my Father's spirit that would not tolerate differences. As a young adult I expressed this perception to Papa and I think it may have made some difference."

About his Mother, Dad reflects, "Although she had some aspirations to be a school teacher, she never was able to fulfill that dream. Nonetheless she had several 'pupils,' as all seven of us siblings learned so much sitting at her feet. I was always amazed at her wisdom and her extremely wide range of interests.

And, in spite of all her interests and responsibilities, and in spite of raising seven children, I very fondly remember that she was an excellent listener. She seemed to always find a way to hear each of us children."

Following, in Dad's own words, are five of the most important lessons he gleaned from his parents:

1. A penny saved is a penny earned.
2. Play is okay after work is done.
3. All work and no play make Jack a dull boy.
4. Prayerfulness begets carefulness.
5. If wisdom's ways you'd wisely seek, five things observe with care: To whom you speak, of whom you speak, and how and when and where.

Upon remembering his parents' guidance and direction, Dad writes, "As far as the two people who have made the greatest spiritual impact upon my life, surely none surpass my parents. I learned such great qualities from them. Like Mom, I would love to listen as she listened. Like Papa, I want to stand upon principles and have a purpose-filled life as he demonstrated."

Born a Great Depression-era baby, Dad knew lean and difficult times. Yet, this frugal and resilient farm family made the best of these circumstances and, as a result, learned valuable lessons that served them well throughout their life. Alluding to this frugality, Dad recalls, "Mother was an excellent cook, but frugal. I remember with fondness a particular homemade chicken-corn soup she prepared. There were several times when she had to add extra water to make sure everyone around the table got enough."

The family made do with what they had, and never seemed to purchase any extras. Like many folks of that day and time, life consisted of the basics, if you were lucky. For example, Pop writes: "We never bought a baseball, glove, or bat. Instead, we made our own. This careful and conservative lifestyle continued. Even after the Depression our frugal style did not change."

Yet, in spite of these tough times, Christian and Elsie Kurtz seemed to always amply provide for their family and were able to even enlarge and improve their farming enterprise. Dad records, "My first and only childhood residence was a stone farmhouse across a highway from our dairy barn. We would tend twice a day to the beef and dairy cattle and poultry that provided our family with nutritional and financial resources even when the economy suffered a depression in the 1930s. We often heard about the hardships but never truly realized the same. In fact, during these lean years Papa, with the assistance of a monthly dairy check, built a potato cellar and over it a three-car garage for our produce and transportation needs. We stored a farm truck, a family auto--a Desoto, and space for the hired hand's vehicle. Some of the time that hired hand was our Uncle Jake Kurtz, who was still single at the time. We loved having Uncle Jake around since he didn't seem to mind our begging him to ride with him when he went into town.

Route 23, which ran right past our home, and which was also a major thorough-fare between Philadelphia and Harrisburg, provided speedy access to various points and places. Crossing this busy highway, from farmhouse to barn, sometimes proved tricky and dangerous. Nonetheless, thankfully, all seven Kurtz children survived this hazard without accident. Unfortunately, not all the Kurtz chickens, nor area drivers, fared as well. On one occasion, a gentleman swerved to miss some of our chickens, which had wandered onto the road, whereupon he overturned his vehicle, landing upside down in a creek beneath the highway."

Crossing Highway 23, and travelling Highway 23 might be considered somewhat symbolic of Dad's life. Each and every day, several times per day, he crossed the road from house to barn, where the farm opportunities and responsibilities awaited. Yet, this same road would lead him out of the Conestoga Valley, away from the farm, and into educational pursuits that would ultimately lead to a medical career. Again, alluding to the highway metaphor, Dr. Kurtz's journey into the medical field, like the dash as a young boy across Route 23, required an alert mind, prudent vision, and a courageous spirit.

It was along Highway 23 in the Kurtz farmhouse that Dad actually received inspiration, and caught a vision for, "a world and a calling beyond the farm," partially through visiting missionaries and through one particular relative, who served as a missionary-physician to the country of India.

"In the early 30's," Dad recalls, "new missionaries were assigned to their respective fields of service. They often spoke at our church prior to leaving and were sometimes meal guests at our home. They were admired greatly by Mamma and Papa, so also by us as children."

But none influenced Pop's medical career and calling decision more than Christian David, or C.D., Esch. C.D. was a first cousin to Dad's Grandmother Stoltzfus. She adored and treasured the letters received from her physician cousin in India. Her frequent memories and mentioning of C.D. and his courageous and beneficial medical work; along with her deep appreciation verbalized for his calling, ultimately led to Dad's becoming a doctor. In Pop's own words, "The memory of her deep appreciation for C.D.'s work led me to also choose medicine and seek to find a place of fruitful service."

Dad would hear from his Grandmother Stoltzfus', and others', stories of inspiration and encouragement concerning this cousin medical missionary, bringing help and healing to poor and suffering lepers in India, and already the seeds were planted in a young boy's mind of the medical vocation opportunities that could become a reality in his own life.

And, yet, before this medical calling and crossing could be followed, there were a lot of cows to be fed and milked; a lot more times to cross highway 23 to the barn; and, a lot more family memories to be made.

Most of Dad's growing up years consisted of family, farm, and church. Faith, family and farm work proved to be the "refinery" from which he formulated values and derived guidance; and, from which he found belonging and support.

Of his childhood home, Pop shares, "Papa inherited the property and house from his parents. They had purchased this land from Welch people. The Welch folk constructed these large, limestone houses throughout the Conestoga Valley when their iron mine industries prospered. I loved the many rooms to explore in our house, including the attic and basement areas. But my favorite room was the kitchen. There I put on my shoes on a cold morning, seated on the bake oven ledge. There we had family meals, family guests and conversations with the crank-type telephone nearby. There we played games--checkers, Chinese checkers, Bible Lotto, Bible Travel Log, drove by hand our toys around the table, and even played ping pong on that same table. I also did creative projects and homework assignments around our kitchen table."

There were also many music memories made together by Pop's family-of-origin. Dad writes: "My first exposure to singing, most certainly, was the nursery rhymes that occupied Mother as she rocked me to sleep, such as 'Rock-a-bye Baby in the Tree-top.' I remember being fascinated and thrilled when she came to the part of this song which related, 'When the bough breaks the cradle will fall and down comes baby, cradle, and all,' as she would quickly lower me in her arms to emulate the falling motion. I also remember my pacifist Mama, ironically, singing, 'Taffy was a Welshman, Taffy was a thief. Taffy came to my house and stole a leg of beef. I went to Taffy's house, Taffy was in bed. I took the marrow bone and broke Taffy's head.'

But church music was the major influence. Four-part harmony without instrumental accompaniment was the only accepted pattern in our conservative Mennonite community. It was believed that no one person should be unnecessarily noticed nor stand out in a crowd, as this was a conviction of Amish and some conservative Mennonite groups, who were convinced that this behavior would find one guilty of the worst sin - - PRIDE. For this reason 'showy' numbers, like solos and quartets were not prevalent. Yet, I do recall one notable exception: C.D. Esch, MD, and his wife on furlough from India, sang a duet which deeply touched our hearts in a particular worship service. The title of this song was, 'The Whole World is Dying for a Little Bit of Love.'

Even a classical music ensemble, meeting regularly in a rented church was perceived as a threat to the congregational expression of one collective voice of the church and was prevailed upon to disband! But we did have midweek singing schools and invited talented musicians from counties east and west to offer a series of vocal lessons, usually shaped notes, with a wide variety of compositions, but no solo parts as I recall."

Many years later, the five grown Kurtz brothers, now with nephews and nieces of their own, became a singing quintet known as "The Uncles." For many years they sang at church and social events, sometimes traveling hundreds of miles to share their gift of song. Through the years they shared their music ministry at scores of venues. They also produced some musical

CDs, which included some of their own original compositions. Among these recorded originals was included Elam's "Where Thou Goest," which was written in honor of Michael and Karen's marriage. The lyrics to this song are included below:

"Where Thou Goest"

1. Three from Moab grief to quell, solace sought in Israel; Widowhood had taken toll, returned in pain of soul.

Chorus: Where thou goest I will go, where thou dwellest, I will dwell. Where thou goest I will go, and I will dwell with thee.

2. Boaz was a man of God, served his town and tilled the sod; Rahab's worthy son indeed, a friend to those in need.

3. Singing these in Bethelehem, Boaz joining in with them; Songs of Moses and a lamb, redemption's brave acclaim.

4. Bitter life in bitter strand, better life in pleasant land; Choices Ruth could now command for Moab and this man.

5. Gleaning these in Boaz fields, sharing soon his bounteous yields; Joy of kin and joy of clan, returned to Ruth again.

6. From that joy there came a peace, from God's grace a sweet release; From that love a sacred line that reaches to our time.

7. Songs of Moses and the Lamb, lyrics, psalms, at David's hand; Love-songs and the wise man's truth, are the cradle touch of Ruth!

Continuing with the topic of music in his elementary school years Pop remembers, "Our public school system was encouraged by concerned school board members to have the entire student body learn the rudiments of vocal music. Special music teachers for all the classes also brought record players to teach music appreciation. Each teacher and class had morning exercises consisting of a variety of selections from a "Golden Book" with usually a classmate with piano skills in accompaniment, a scripture reading, and the reciting of 'The Pledge of Allegiance.' I discovered some students were uncertain about saying the Pledge, and for a while I was also unsure, until our Mennonite principal, Noah Good, rationalized that compliance with this action was okay since the Pledge itself declares 'liberty and justice for all.'

Each Christmas Season the four rooms with two grades in each had a major assembly with a musical play presented. The one I recall best happened after my britches had ripped in the seat and I hid myself in the back row as best I could during the recitation in which of all things we shouted out, 'Don't bust out your pantaloons and don't wear out your shoes!'"

As much as Dad loved the educational environment, and thrived at school, it would not be many hours, that particular embarrassing day, and all days, until he would be slipping on his work clothes and his farm shoes. The livestock and the crops would not wait. There was work to be done. And, after all, Dad was the oldest son and eldest sibling, and one day he would take over the family farm. For several years Pop faithfully, and competently, labored on the Route 23 farm. Dad remembers, "Papa's neighbor, Levi Stoltzfus, offered to sale the farm adjacent to our farm, perceiving that the five growing sons may need room to grow. For three or more years I farmed that dairy and poultry resource residing at the home place and travelling to chore-duties by a used 1934 Chevy, or my first bicycle. I saved enough money from my farming years to finish medical school training and get to North Carolina both penniless and debtless."

But, pursuing a dream, in 1947, at age twenty-three, Dad left the Route 23 farm and made his crossing to Lebanon Valley College. It was during these undergraduate days that Dad began dating Orpah Mae Horst, from Reading, Pennsylvania. Dad's family and the Horst family knew each other from church worship services and special singings.

Elam and Orpah's love for, and commitment to, one another grew slowly and steadily. When Dad was asked the question, "When did you know that Mom was the "one and only one" for you?" he responded, "The conviction was gradual, but strong." They spent over two and one-half years dating and seeing each other.

During these years of courting much of the time consisted of a long-distance romance. While going through Pop's personal items, upon his death, the family located a large box of letters which contained many of the love letters exchanged by Orpah and Elam during these years, with Mom being in Pennsylvania and Dad attending school at EMC and later at LVC. Excerpts of these love letters include:

> December 13, 1949
> Dearest Orpah,
> There are a few letters to write in the near future. This is one of them, the last one this year. The number following is not large and then we will finally be together!
> I neglected earlier to mention to you about the nice printing in one of the recent envelopes you sent. You had

written "Wedding Bells." I am very glad you too look forward to a home of your own.

Perhaps because of the quietness of the evening......I think I must hear you, but you are far away. So I end my letter writing to you in 1949, and give you my wishes for a Merry Christmas and a Happy New Year, and with it a wish that I may help to make them just so.

Fondly, Elam

March 7, 1950
To the one I love,

Shall I write your name in the heading? Who else could it be but you, Orpah?

I am living in pleasant memories of the times spent together over the holiday season, especially recalling the day of which you said that we made a good beginning for the New Year.

I told Harold a while ago I am looking forward to married life. More especially, I am looking forward to sharing everything as long as we live.

From the one who loves,
Elam

March 21, 1950
To the One I Love,

It seems like a long time since I wrote a letter to you, I guess it seems long because we didn't write any last week, and it won't be long until we won't need to write any to each other.

How are things coming along with the trailer? Did you have it moved yet? I am anxious to get it cleaned up and ready to live in it. I thought maybe Mother and I could come up some time next week, I know Mother is anxious to see it.

I must say goodnight, it is my bed time. Each day
that passes by brings us closer to the day when we will
be together.

Love, Orpah

Dad proposed to Mom toward the end of 1949. Reminiscing, Pop
shares, "I proposed to Orpah on 13th Street in Reading, Pennsylvania.
We took a walk and stopped on the front steps of a school building, where
I asked for her hand in marriage. She said 'Yes.' That clinched it! I then
proceeded to ask Papa Horst, who gave his blessing."

Mom and Dad were married in Reading, Pennsylvania on April 1st,
also Dad's birthday, 1950, in a Mennonite church on the corner of 12th and
Windsor Streets. Recalling their wedding day, Pop notes, "Special wedding
music was provided by a singing group standing in the church balcony. The
presiding pastor was Bishop Paul Graybill. Rev. Graybill arrived late to the
ceremony due to getting caught at a train crossing. Orpah's brother, Leon,
came to the rescue and led congregational singing until the pastor arrived.
When the preacher finally showed up we continued with the wedding. In
spite of the rough beginning, all went well."

Mom and Dad travelled to Indiana for their honeymoon during a break
in college classes. In her Bridal Book, Mom records, "We spent the first
night of our honeymoon together in our little home, which was a twenty-
eight foot Liberty house trailer. On Sunday morning we enjoyed fellowship
with a congregation near Cleveland. On Monday we travelled as far as
Helena, Ohio, some of the journey following along Lake Erie.

On Tuesday we came to Goshen Indiana and met some friends there.
We then made our headquarters at my brother Paul's home. Thursday we
travelled east as far as East Liverpool. Friday we followed the Ohio River
southward and then we drove to Scottdale, Pennsylvania. We returned to
our home on Saturday."

Elam and Orpah set up housekeeping in the mobile home adjacent to
the Lebanon Valley College campus. The view out of the kitchen window
was a neighbor's trailer. The view from their living room was a school and
tennis court. A path led from their trailer to a community outhouse that
served as their lavatory.

From LVC the couple moved to Cleveland, Ohio, in 1951, where
Elam enrolled as a first year medical student at Case Western Reserve.
Mom and Dad were able to purchase a home in the Bedford Heights area
of Cleveland. Payments were made each month through the assistance
of Mom's part time jobs and through the rent monies received from the
housing of two 1 - W workers, conscientious objectors who served their

country in alternate ways other than the military. Of this home Dad shares, "We couldn't find a place to rent in Cleveland and with Orpah obviously pregnant, we needed a place pretty bad. On the very street of the church we chose to attend a couple was frustrated about how to remodel their house and gladly got rid of their 'problem' by selling the Louis Road house to us. We settled for $8,000.00 and early occupancy. We made necessary improvements on the house and changed from coal heating to city gas and added an artificial stone front. Our two thousand dollars in improvements was recovered when we later sold the home. Five years of medical training and the rest of summer school months made full use of this purchase. We sold the property for what we had invested, and of course we also lived rent-free!"

Elam and Orpah also became very involved in the Friendship Mennonite Church, just down the street from their residence, where Pastor Dale Nafsinger and his wife became good friends of Dad and Mom.

While living in Cleveland their first child, Karen Joyce, was born on October 2nd, 1951. They continued living in Cleveland, Dad going to medical school and doing his internship, graduating from Case Western Reserve School of Medicine in 1955. In the summer of 1955, following a battery of fertility tests the prior year, Orpah and Elam's second child, Michael David was born. Exactly one year later, June 27th, 1956, the family of four moved to the Appalachian Mountains of North Carolina to begin a brand new life--crossing over the mountains and crossing into a new and different culture from the one in which they had been raised and accustomed.

I asked Dad shortly before he died how he had managed to make the transition from North to South, from Pennsylvania's orthodox Mennonite culture to Southern Bible Belt culture? And, without hesitation, he pointed to Mom, who was seated around the kitchen table with us, and he replied, "Your mother. She helped it happen....couldn't have done it without her."

I knew what he meant. Pop was the pioneer, vision, big-picture guy of the team. But he knew he could not pursue his dreams and goals without Mom. He was the big-picture guy, but Mom kept Dad's feet firmly planted on the ground. She was the pragmatic one. She could pull off the social conversations. She could manage the money and balance the books. She could instruct him which clothing matched and which clothes to put on. She could put her foot down when the vision possibly "went into orbit."

All four of us siblings to this day give thanks for the love, support, and guidance that this solid marital dyad provided for each and every one of us throughout each stage of life. The love and commitment that Mom and

Dad possessed and displayed for each other provided a security that yielded deep roots of connection, and which enabled wings of independence.

Elam and Orpah were a team from the very beginning. Their gifts and skills complemented one another. Their love which began slow and steady evolved into a treasured tapestry of respect and faithfulness. Located in one of Dad's diaries was a page which contained his ideas on what it takes for a husband and wife to maintain a healthy marriage. It reads "Resolve to faithfulness; Cultivate and express admiration for your partner's traits; and, lovingly care for the descendants." Pertaining to this last idea, I recall Dad often saying, "The best way for me to love my children is to love their mother."

This philosophy of love we saw manifest in Mom and Dad's faithfulness and commitment; in their romantic bantering; and in their teamwork service and outreach to others. When Dad was asked what event(s), if any, in life had strengthened his belief in prayer? Immediately he responded, "I asked God for the one with whom I could serve Him best. No doubt that major prayer got an answer in Orpah." Mom and Dad shared and showed a love for each other, and for us children, that neither smothered nor isolated. While neither a perfect marriage nor a perfect family, there seemed to be a healthy amount of connection and a functional amount of flexibility so that the result was neither enmeshed dependency nor estranged independency; but, instead a healthy interdependency for all.

Five years after moving to Ashe County, North Carolina a third child, Becky Ann was born at Ashe Memorial Hospital in July of 1961. Then, in 1964 the fourth and final child was born to Orpah and Elam. Kevin John arrived on October 2nd of that same year. The October 2nd date gave the very same birthday to the eldest Kurtz child and to the youngest. With the birth of Kevin the Kurtz family circle was completed.

In 1990 Pop filled out a questionnaire to be included in a publication by writers entitled "Ideas for Families." In this survey he shares the following responses, "The common denominator for successful homes is acceptance. The cement is communication. And, the goal is mothering (nurturing), not smothering." These are three goals that our family, with Mom and Dad's lead, pursued, not perfectly, but persistently. Through this parental and family guidance and effort we crossed over from being individual autonomous agents to being a more cohesive and functional unit. Hopefully through this cohesiveness and teamwork approach there was a multiplication and strengthening of each family member's gifts and skills so that greater effectiveness and good could be facilitated in the larger society. This then affirms that there is a much greater purpose beyond just the single family unit. Theologically and philosophically speaking, a family is never intended by the Creator to be an end in and of it self. Instead, the family is called by God to be a means through which persons may be nurtured and equipped to make a positive impact in the larger world.

Dad taught an altruistic approach to life. He taught this through some verbal teaching, but certainly more so through his actions. No doubt we as Pop's children would say when it comes to Pop "more was caught than taught." Or, put another way, more was conveyed to us through his actions and lifestyle than through mere words. Dad was not big on "big talking." He would rather see a sermon than hear a sermon. I find that I learned much more from observing Dad's life than from his words of instruction.

Having said this, because Dad was not very adept at small talk, I recall times growing up when I wanted more of this every day dialog with Dad, yet it was neither a big part of his personality nor his style. Dad and I, for example, spoke somewhat different languages. On the Myers-Briggs Temperament Analysis Inventory he was high on the Thinking scale. I was high on the Feeling scale. So, we sometimes spoke a different lingo. Feeling and discerning this "conversation chasm" between the two of us, when I was in my early 30s, I asked Pop to ride with me in my car to the top of one of the local mountains, a mountain we loved and climbed together many times. We stopped at one of the overlooks, looking out over the beautiful Blue Ridge Mountains. And as we sat there I read to him a letter I had written about my love and appreciation for him and how we might try to understand one another's language a bit better. Then we drove down the mountain listening to Mike and the Mechanics singing "In the Living Years" without saying a word to one another. We pulled into his driveway, getting out of the car in silence. Before we went into the house Pop turned and looked at me and said, "Maybe your Dad can work harder on this communication thing." And from this meeting on the mountain came a "crossing" in our relationship. It was not magical. There was not a momentous change. Yet, something happened, whether inside me or inside both of us. For our relationship became more of a man-to-man relationship than ever before. There followed a renewed respect for, and a better understanding of, one another that was to last until he parted.

Personally, this father-son experience was further evidence, and one example, of an evolving, growing family life that mandated time, effort and involvement with one another, with the glue being commitment. Becky shares: "Dad was committed to family. Despite his commitment to his vocation, he was also always there for us, his family. He made it a priority to be home every evening at 6pm sharp for family dinner, even if later he had to return to the hospital. We'd often sing, 'I Thank the Lord my Maker,' as grace before dinner. And every evening we had family devotion time.

In addition, Thursday was sacred for Dad. It was family day. So after school we had activities as a family, whether we played games, took hikes, or watched documentaries."

In responding to the prior mentioned family survey which asked, "What kind of ordinary, anytime fun does your family, have together," Pop responded, "We have gone camping together, sleeping in a tent and then following that with a canoe trip. We have taken many hikes over trails in the beautiful Blue Ridge Mountains where we live. We also play a lot of games as a family. For example, we play ping-pong and tennis, chess, checkers, Sorry, Uncle Wiggly, Dutch Blitz, and various word games.

Dad also answered a survey question asking "What traditions have you developed for special occasions?" "We have a tradition of gathering the family together at a beach cabin or a mountain resort each summer for a week. We, for years, have gathered together for Thanksgiving and Christmas holidays. A circular letter has also been employed at times--a letter that gets passed from household to household sharing and adding the latest news. We attend graduations and artistic performances and sporting events as they occur. As the years have gone by I have taken pictures of each child and their particular interests and have put together a slide show for each. It has become a tradition to look at these slides at least once a year, spawning various comments and much laughter!"

To the question "Do you practice any form of worship or family prayers," Dad shared, "We always offered a prayer prior to our meals. Sometimes we prayed a prayer such as 'God is great. God is good. Let us thank Him for our food. By His hand we all are fed. Give us, Lord, our daily bread. Amen.' Other times at table we took turns praying extemporaneous prayers and sometimes even singing our prayer. As to devotions, we attempted to have a family altar time each evening before going to bed. Time constraints, as well as attention deficit, were sometimes issues. In order to help with this we kept our devotional time brief and tried to be creative in our approach. We rotated the leadership of family worship with resources such as, "Go Till You Guess," "Know Your Bible," "Bible Story Book," and "Words for Christian Athletes." Informal and impromptu dramas were also encouraged, sometimes acting out a Bible story for the other family members to guess."

When friends or guests were in our home these devotional times continued, uninterrupted, much to the chagrin of teenagers, who hoped for a hiatus from such. However, looking back each of us grown children remembers with appreciation and fondness these important centering times. One medical student who lived with our family during his externship wrote a letter of appreciation and thanks to our family.

Dear Friends,

One gift that you gave to me this summer might not have been so apparent to you. It was the greatest joy to see and to be a part of a Christian home such as yours. Your devotional times set an example that I'll never forget. The dedication of your family to the people and the Mennonite Church on Little Horse Creek was an inspiration to me. It made me renew again my hope that the home Dale (fiancé) and I will soon have will be as beautiful and as Christian as yours is.

In my opinion, you folks are among the greatest people I have ever known. You gave and you gave and you gave. I'll never be able to repay you. Just know that your investment in my life is, and will be, a lasting one. It is one I'll never forget. Thank you for caring about people.

Love, John

To the question, "How did you give your children individual attention," came this reply, "Orpah and I tried to treat each child with fairness and with interest in, and support of, their respective personal pursuits. Our intent was not to live our expectations through them, but rather support them in finding their own way. I had the privilege of taking a special travel opportunity with each child. Orpah and I took our first child to Haiti. Likewise our second child accompanied me on a medical mission trip to Haiti for two weeks together. Our third child traveled on my motorcycle with me to Nova Scotia." This trip was remembered by Becky, "Sometimes we learned about the purpose of our journeys through Dad's readings. Dad and I took a trip to Nova Scotia in 1979, and part of our quest was to find the land of Evangeline. He had been inspired by the Longfellow poem. I sat on the back of his motorcycle for two weeks of travel. On our way we visited Boston where I learned the hard way that not all Chinese restaurants accept credit cards or traveler's checks. While Dad returned to the hotel for cash, he left me as hostage."

"Our fourth child and I rode our motorcycles to Yellowstone National Park, covering over 5,500 miles in fifteen days," concludes Pop.

Addressing the survey question as to "What vacations have you taken as a family," Pop writes, "We were able to take three generations of our family to Europe. This was one way to get away and get together. We also took trips to the following locations: A family vacation across America to California and back; Yellowstone; Florida; Charleston, S.C.; Niagara Falls;

Haiti; Red Lake, Canada, where we flew into a wilderness mission outpost landing on water in a pontoon plane; and, Monhegan Island off the coast of Maine. We also took regular family vacations to the beach as well as taking trips to Pennsylvania to be with grandparents and other relatives."

On many of these road trips we children recall, in addition to being hot, tired, and engaged in backseat territorial sibling arguments, the fun times of Dad and Mom challenging us to a game of "Alphabet Races"-- employing billboards and license plates to see who could first locate the entire alphabet. We would also play the "cattle game"--seeing who could get to one-hundred cows first, on their side of the road. Then, rules stated, if we ever came across a cemetery on our side, pointed out by our "opponents" we would be required to "bury" all our cattle and start our count all over. When the games finished, if Mom were driving, Dad would often read age-appropriate books to us.

Travel was recreational as well as educational for Dr. Kurtz. He would sometimes allow us children to miss some school for travel experiences because as he often affirmed, "Travel is an education like no other." Since travel meant so much to him and to our entire family, perhaps the most special trip of all was a vacation that occurred just five months before Dad died.

Karen relates, "When I asked Dad how he'd like to celebrate his and Mom's upcoming 60th wedding anniversary, he replied, 'I'd like to go to New York City or Moscow.' We couldn't quite figure out how to make his Moscow dream work, but we four children made one of his dreams come true by taking Mom and Dad to New York City for their anniversary. We are so grateful to him for inspiring us with his dream so that our original family of six could experience a most memorable time together! Dad was a dreamer, but so often, his dreams were a gift to others."

To the final survey question on the family questionnaire, which inquired, "Any other comments," Dad reflected, "Voluntary services have been modeled and encouraged for our children--to freely contribute gifts and services to humanity and society. We have likewise supported educational opportunities and endeavors, as well as chosen careers, by our children. In an autograph album, which my Mother presented to me in 1956, she wrote, 'I have no greater joy than to see my children walk in truth.' This joy experience continues even this month that I write as our first child is undertaking the beginning of a Self Help store; our second child held revival meetings in a nearby church; our third child is an advocate for the elderly; and our fourth child follows my career choice."

For Dad family relationships were always important, requiring a continual investment of time and involvement. He would often say to us grown children upon a visit home, "Thanks for taking time to come see your Mother and me. We appreciate it so much!"

Over the years as we children all grew and changed through the experiences and seasons of life Pop remained a stabilizer and a support in all our crossings and transitioning.

* *

From the family farm with seven siblings along Route 23…. to the 28-foot trailer where he and Mom first set up housekeeping…. to the home on Louis Road in Cleveland…. then to living in Ashe County, with eventually four children…..through each and every one of these crossings family was always a high priority.

Dad came from a long line of love and through Dad and Mom's love and nurture that long line continues in and through succeeding generations. As noted earlier, family for Dad was not an end in and of itself, but rather a vehicle and means through which Christ and humankind are served. The very last question asked of Pop in a journal entitled "A Father's Legacy," and to which he responded, was, "What advice about life do you want your family to remember?" He replied, "Whatever life brings the central person and central purpose is Jesus."

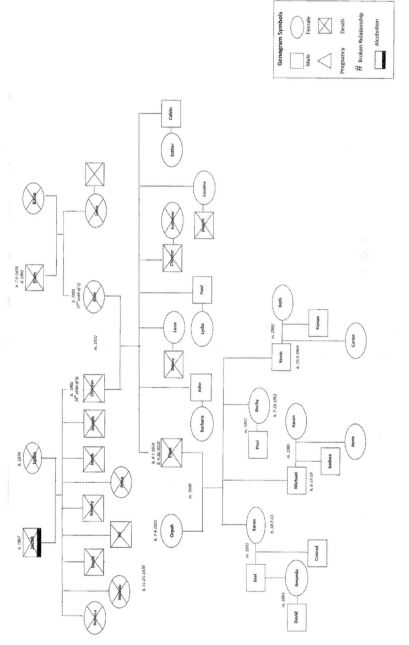

Elam S. Kurtz genogram

As for me and my house, we will serve the Lord.
Joshua 24:15

Address:
Annville, Penna.

Elam and Orpah started house-keeping in this mobile home

dinner guests

Louis Road home in Cleveland

The Uncles

Family trip to NYC—November 2009

Central Park's Tavern on the Green—Mom and Dad's 60th anniversary trip

Gravesite for Christian and Elsie Kurtz, Elverson, Pa.

CHAPTER FIVE

GEOGRAPHICAL CROSSINGS

*"Great things are done when men and mountains meet." –
William Blake*

Dad loved to explore and experience different places and various cultures. Whether leaving the Lancaster County, Pennsylvania farm for college; traveling from Cleveland, Ohio to Ashe County, North Carolina to establish a medical practice; or, taking treks to many lands around the world, Dad's pioneering spirit was frequently activated and pursued.

Travels were many and varied. During the 1960s and 1970s Dad made a couple of medical mission trips to Haiti. On one of those trips Mom and Karen accompanied him. On the other occasion I as a young teenager made this trek to this poverty-stricken, oppressed tiny nation.

As mentioned before, travels were always an adventure with Pop, and this Haitian trip certainly was no exception to that rule. The day after we arrived on Haitian soil political unrest broke out. Because of this unrest, usual and ordinary public transportation was shut down, to further secure the capital city of Port-au-Prince where Dad and I had found lodging for the first night of our trip.

Dad was undaunted by this transportation "shut down," and refused to be denied the opportunity to make our way to the assigned mission site located on the northern coast of Haiti. Since there was no bus service, Dad took us down to a local port and there we located a thirty-foot rickety sailboat with a small and questionable-looking crew that was willing to take us near our desired destination for a few dollars.

I will never forget this boat ride on the Caribbean Sea as long as I live! The ride was to take six hours. Yet, due to a fierce storm at sea, the trip took twenty-two hours! The old sailboat rocked and creaked in the fierce storm. I have never been as sea sick, or as homesick, in my entire life. As a young teen I made my peace with my Creator on board that sailing vessel and vowed to never do anything like this again if only I could find land under my feet.

Pop and I made it to the medical clinic where we worked for ten days serving the desperately sick prior to our return to the United States. Due to Pop's persistence the mission was accomplished. When the land crossing was denied, we crossed by sea.

Another trip included a family travel to Red Lake, Ontario in Canada to visit Dad's first cousin, Lydia Kurtz, who was a missionary to the Indians in that rural territory. The only way we could get to this missionary outpost was by pontoon plane. It was an awesome adventure to land by plane on the lake, surrounded by small huts, wildlife and dense forests.

Karen reminisces about this Canadian adventure, "We spent a day boating on the lake, planning to have the fish we caught for lunch. Even though Lydia assured us that everyone caught fish in this lake, we never caught a single one. By lunch time, we stopped on an island and ate the only food we had along--dried moose liver! It was so disgusting I couldn't bear to eat it. When Lydia wasn't looking, I tossed it over my shoulder."

The remainder of our time was spent assisting cousin Lydia in her daily tasks and after one week enabling her to go back to America, having completed her term of service.

Dr. Kurtz made additional trips to Russia, Europe, and several mission trips to Jamaica, often with Ashe County citizen Jackie Blackburn. In 2000 Elam and his two sons Michael and Kevin shared a pilgrimage to the Holy Land. There they spent ten days tracing the steps of Jesus while appreciating some father-son connecting time.

Yet, of all the trips Dad had taken, one that held extra special significance for him, as it related to his vocation, was his journey to India during 2003. For this was a retracing the steps of his medical relative, Dr. C.D. Esch, the one who had inspired Elam as a young boy on a Pennsylvania dairy farm to envision becoming a doctor.

The following article, which chronicles Dad's India trek, appeared in a Reading, Pennsylvania newspaper in January of 2004:

PASSAGE TO INDIA: Physician Retraces Steps

"As a boy in the early 1930s, Dr. Elam S. Kurtz was struck that his grandmother was so captivated by a letter from her missionary cousin in India. Kurtz, who grew up on a farm near Morgantown, recalled that his Amish grandmother Katie Beiler Stoltzfus wasn't the type to show emotion. 'I remember clearly her reading this letter and her admiration,' Kurtz said. 'Grandmother was never expressive, but that was one time she expressed deep feelings, and that impressed me.'

Kurtz, who recently retired from his medical practice in North Carolina, said he owes his long and fulfilling career in part to that letter from Christian David Esch, a pioneer missionary physician to India. In September 2003, Kurtz, age 79, traveled to India to retrace the footsteps of his late, distant relative, known as C.D.

'I went over with the idea of this being somewhat of a pilgrimage, an ancestral pilgrimage,' said Kurtz, who returned in October to his home in Ashe County, N.C. 'I went over with the idea of thanking the Esch family when I returned for giving C.D. to us.'

The American-born Esch was orphaned at age eight by a train wreck in Lancaster, Pa. He and his eight siblings were sent to live with relatives in Lancaster and Berks counties. Esch went to live with a cousin, Levi Beiler in Caernarvon Township, and worked as a farmhand for Kurtz's paternal grandparents, Jacob and Lydia Mast Kurtz.

As Kurtz later would be by him, Esch was inspired by a missionary physician to India to become a doctor. After completing his medical training, Esch went to India, where he helped establish the Dhamtari Hospital, a 300-bed facility in central India. He spent two decades in India as a missionary physician with the Mennonite Church before his death in a swimming accident near Dhamtari in 1931.

Kurtz said he doesn't recall ever meeting Esch, although Esch and his wife, Mina, visited the Conestoga Amish-Mennonite congregation in Morgantown in 1928. Still, he considers Esch to be his mentor.

An arthritic knee convinced Kurtz at age 21 that he had no future as a dairy farmer. 'When I was faced with a change in my career, it came to mind how my grandmother felt about her cousin,' he said. 'So I decided to pursue the field of medicine. So I give him credit in absentia for my decision to go into medicine.'

Kurtz admitted that part of his reason for traveling to India was to visit the spot where Esch perished and to shed some light on his mysterious death. Kurtz went to the reservoir about 10 miles from Dhamtari where Esch met his doom in 1931. He also visited Esch's burial site. He met Mennonite Bishop P.J. Malaghar, 83, who was able to describe in detail how Esch was hurled over the dam breast and into rocks. Kurtz said it was satisfying to hear the bishop's account because it convinced him that Esch's death was accidental. He had heard accounts that Esch was stricken by a heart attack. 'They took nets there to try to fish the body out,' Kurtz said. 'He must have been jammed in the rocks at the dam. If it had been a heart attack or the bends, he would have surfaced readily.'

He got a sense that Esch's death was a tremendous loss to the community. His respect grew after hearing the bishop explain Esch's role in establishing Dhamtari Hospital, which is set to become just the third Christian medical school in India. 'It increased my admiration to think he was able to build this hospital in the first year he was there,' Kurtz said. 'While we were there, you could see how much the people got behind presenting the institution and how committed they are to make the changes needed to become a medical school. The government is encouraging the venture, which would be a catalyst for economic development in the region,' Kurtz explained.

Accompanying Kurtz on the tour of India was Dr. Joseph J. Duerksen, a Kansas anesthesiologist who was born in India of American missionary parents. Kurtz said he was fortunate to be able to travel with someone with Duerksen's connections. Kurtz likened the region, which is India's most productive rice-growing area, to Lancaster County.

Keeping to his promise, Kurtz wrote to Esch family members to report on the trip and express his gratitude for what Esch meant to his life. In a way, Kurtz's journey has only begun. He plans to use slides and memories of his tour to encourage others to support the medical school at Dhamtari Hospital."

Dad approached the India trip and each of the previously mentioned travels as an educational opportunity.....learning more about his family as in the C.D. Esch case; or, learning more about his human family--various cultures and different styles of life. Dad's mind and heart were so open to traveling and learning. Travel was in his blood and he was ready for a trip on just a moment's notice.

On one occasion Dad was asked, "What four things would you never leave behind on a trip and explain why?" He answered, as a doctor and health-conscious individual, "My medicine box with blood pressure and cholesterol medication;" As a Christian, "My Bible for guidance;" As an explorer crossing many miles, "My driver's license for transportation;" And as a person who treasured relationships and experiences, "My memories for myself, my family and my friends."

* *

As wonderful as each and all of these trips were to Dad, and as much as he enjoyed these travel experiences most of all he loved the people and the land known as Ashe County.

Becky remembers, "Dad loved Ashe County. In 1970, we took the Kurtz version of National Lampoon's "Vacation" adventure - - All six of us piled into the Jeep Wagoneer to head west. We drove across the entire country, stopping to visit friends and relatives along the way until we made it to Disneyland. We saw so many amazing places: Yellowstone, the Grand Canyon, and the Painted Desert. But as we drove into Ashe County, after driving thousands of miles, Dad said, 'We saw lots of beautiful places on this trip, but, you know, none of them are as beautiful as Ashe County.'"

Dad knew so well the communities, the mountains, and the roads of his beloved County. He spent many times and hours crossing the terrain of Ashe whether in car or on motorcycle, bicycle, or by foot. Once again Becky shares: "Dad was committed to exploration. If we went one route to get to our destination, Dad would insist on returning by another route. He always wanted to explore the back roads of Ashe County and would take turns down unknown roads just to see where they would lead. We often got lost and he adamantly refused to ask directions, but with his good sense of direction, he knew we'd always eventually find our way home--and we would have explored a whole new part of Ashe County."

For more than fifty years Dr. Kurtz crossed over and traversed the valleys and mountains of his home, the Appalachian landscape with which he had fallen in love. From the very beginning he had found a people and a place with which he could identify and relate. Speaking of his very first exploratory trip to Ashe County Dad writes, "Elmer Eberly drove Orpah and me to see first-hand North Carolina's practice opportunity taking our 1950 Mercury while I rested on the floorboard. I had been up all night treating a case of diabetic acidosis. Interns didn't get to visit their next appointments in those days, so an understanding supervisor, Dr. Nichols, who believed I'd learn a lot from mountain medical experiences, urged me to take the time to travel the 500 miles.

At Mr. Koontz' Gulf Station I made the first phone call person-to-person to my next physician-colleague, Dean C. Jones, Sr., MD, and I knew at once he was a kindly person. That contrasted sharply with the rough treatment interns had from the attending surgeons in the big city. Working with the Ashe Memorial Hospital staff was so refreshing! For example, I noticed early on while assisting Dr. Jones how efficiently and compassionately nurse-assistant Mary Wilcox expedited the surgeon's every move, verses my experience with St. Luke's (Cleveland, Ohio) nurses who were often difficult to locate and seldom cheerful in their disposition. I was eagerly anticipating serving my country in North Carolina!"

Climb Every Mountain

Dad possessed not only a deep love for the Ashe County Mountains but also a great first hand knowledge of the County's various ranges and peaks. He led many folks on hiking experiences throughout the area. I recall accompanying him on numerous hikes. We spent hours on the hills climbing such mountains as Phoenix, the Notches, Three Top, the Peak, the Bluff, Listening Rock, Long Meadow and Little Phoenix. But probably our favorite of all climbs, and the one we ascended most frequently was Mount Jefferson. We climbed Mount Jefferson at least a dozen times together, sometimes taking other persons with us.

There were two main attractions on our ascent to the summit of Mount Jefferson that we always loved to encounter. One was Fat Man's Squeeze. Fat Man's Squeeze was so named because it was a narrow but deep chasm that one had to jump across in order to continue the climb on the trail to the top. As a young boy Dad would encourage me to make the jump across this chasm into his waiting arms. As I got older the jump seemed like a much easier feat.

The second exciting stop on the climb was the "slave cave," which was reported to be an actual hiding out location of the Underground Railroad system during the Civil War era. I always loved to sit for a few minutes in the coolness of the cave and imagine the slaves and their helpers finding shelter and safety on their flight to freedom.

Dad reflects on the mountains of Ashe, "Here in Ashe County, I am surrounded by beautiful mountains waiting to be explored. The most intriguing may be the cave on Mt. Jefferson with Underground Railroad tradition--runaway slaves seeking their freedom! On one of my nearly 20 mountain hikes to the cave I was accompanied by a Methodist pastor with American Indian heritage who identified diggings on the mountainside for 'sang,' locally the name for ginseng.

Among the many mountains I have hiked: Mt. Jefferson, The Peak at Creston, probably our tallest; Mount Paddy that faces West Jefferson; Little Phoenix; Big Phoenix; Bluff Mountain, now in the protection of The Nature Conservancy--and often ridden by trail bike; the Pond Mountain area even into Tennessee to the Laurel Bloomery; and hiking down with Grady Shepherd to the twin falls on the Gentry Creek, where a narrow gauge railroad once harvested lumber.

Eastward the Blue Ridge Parkway offers accessible walkways and scenic overlooks. This roadway has repeatedly been included in the annual bicycle rides.

One medical student rode with me on mountain bikes to the Johnnessy Rock up on the Three-top Mountain. We passed by what was once the residence of Monroe Jones and his son, Paul. Rescuers had sought to help them in the Big Snow of 1960. They both had declined to leave their mountain home. To access the sawmill road onto this property we lifted our bikes across the wire fence. Behind us was the valley up Buffalo Creek leading to the Bluff Mountain.

A local radiologist, Robert Groves, and I found the entire hike of the Three Top included two days with both days ending down the steep slopes into the Buffalo Community. En route we passed by the 'Elephant Rock,' and the nearly flat site where Rev. Gary Richardson and I once took our tents and camped for a night."

Dad not only admired the majestic Blue Ridge Mountains from a distance; in addition, he explored and experienced those mountains first-hand and up-close. The many crossings and admirations of these gorgeous and challenging peaks soon enabled the mountains to become a part of his soul and a part of his soles!

Crossings on Bicycle

Dad found great enjoyment and recreational diversion, as well as physical exercise, in bicycle riding. He comments, "After moving into a home at the foot of Mount Jefferson, I discovered that with the multiple gears of a mountain bike I could master many roads and hills of Ashe County, including the climb up Mount Jefferson itself. A Tour du Pont ride had passed my own Lansing office one year which included Lance Armstrong. I was likewise inspired by rides with Appalachian State University faculty riders taking on our North Carolina Green Cove to the Virginia Green Cove on Ashe County secondary roads. I tried repeatedly to complete a ride up Rich Hill above the community center but could not get past a turn at a cemetery at the pavement's end.

Next I chose the Flat Rock Road near the Shatley Springs Resort but had repeated drive chain breakdowns. But then I found a better, more convenient ride for my purposes--the three mile road up Mount Jefferson. And it was on this road I trained repeatedly until I could ride non-stop the entire three miles and achieve the 1100 feet elevation of change. Family and friends gathered round on the day I made my 1,000[th] - ride up the summit."

Pop's bicycle interest had influence upon the entire Kurtz family. For well over two decades, and continuing today, the family has taken an annual bike ride usually on the Virginia Creeper Trail. Our seventeen mile ride begins at White Top, Virginia and meanders from there down to Damascus, Virginia. Into his eighties Dad was still making this family bike trek.

Kevin shares, "Dad loved his bicycle exploits. His riding over 1000 trips to the top of Mount Jefferson State Park Road over the course of many years, after a diagnosis of heart disease in the early 1980s, is well remembered. Dad has inspired our family to bike the Creeper Trail annually during October. Reflecting on our last bike trip that Dad made in 2004, we may be the only family in that trail's history to have ages ranging from my 5-year-old son Kenan to Dad at age 80, biking from White Top Station to Damascus at the same time."

One of Dr. Kurtz's bicycle legacies is that of Ashe County's Brutal 100- -a 100-mile bike ride that lives up to its name. From a newspaper article comes the following excerpts on this mountain ride:

Early Days of the Blue Ridge Brutal Bike Ride

"Dr. Elam Kurtz, the beloved Ashe County physician and avid biker, designed the first 100 mile course. It started at Glendale Springs, followed the Blue Ridge Parkway into Virginia, and returned on Highway 16, including the old steel bridge on Highway 16, back to Glendale Springs. Dr. Kurtz and his son Michael rode their bikes on the route as a trial run.

When the ride and lots of fundraising resulted in the Ashe Civic Center's being constructed, the ride and the route were changed so that the ride began at the Civic Center's present location on Highway 221. The new route, which was used until 1999, headed south on 221, all the way to Highway 421, then headed north on the Parkway. The first section of the Parkway was a 2 ½ mile ascent. Richard Shepherd manned a rest stop at the overlook at the top of the hill. He says that the riders were exhausted when they reached him. He provided drinks, cookies, and fruit to the riders. The hard core bikers proceeded after a short break, but many of the riders took a rest there. A few hours later, Dr. Kurtz would arrive on his bike.

Dr. Kurtz was very enthusiastic about a race up to the top of Mt. Jefferson. He named it the Assault on Mt. Jefferson. It took place on the Friday evening before the annual race on Saturday. Today riders are offered an opportunity to assault Mt. Jefferson after the 100 mile ride on Saturday.

Dr. Kurtz continued his active participation in planning and riding in the Brutal. He rode the entire 100 miles during the first three years of the ride. In 1992, he came in with a time of 10:46:00 for 39th place. His last year was 2006 when he was 82 years old and biked 27 miles to the Northwest Trading Post, where the SAG Wagon picked him up and brought him back to the Civic Center. In 2008 he looked back to the first ride and noted that the original goal of the course was to 'expose the riders to the scenery of Ashe County and find paved roads that you could use to circumvent the county, which wasn't easy.' He added that the course was meant to be as challenging as possible. 'Many a rider who has ridden elsewhere says this is properly named 'Brutal,' he said."

In addition to crossing the Ashe Mountains by bicycle Pop also loved motorcycle riding. He purchased his first motorcycle in the early 1970s during the gas shortage to make house calls. I recall Dad's first two off-road motorcycles were 175 and 250 Yamahas. He and I, as well as others, spent hours covering the saw mill roads on Phoenix Mountain, travelling over Listening Rock on the way to Laurel Bloomery, TN., and several other rides.

From the off-road bikes Dad graduated to a Yamaha 1200 touring bike which he rode to Yellowstone Park, along with Kevin who road a bike of his own. Of this specific travel Dad records, "Our son, Kevin, in growing up, was perceived by his mother, Orpah, to need a closer relationship with me. His elder brother had had a transforming experience with his father-son relationship on a short-term, two-week Christian Mission trip to Haiti. So when Kevin offered to ride to California on a motorcycle we seized the opportunity. Kevin insisted on his own two wheels which became available upon purchase of a Yamaha 750cc Midnight Special, previously owned by Elliott Osowitt. We settled for a lesser distance to the Yellowstone National Park and completed 5,555 miles in 15 days and similarly achieved a cemented father-son bonding."

Once he purchased the touring bike Dad was hooked on the "hawg."

He even convinced Mom to ride several long trips with him until she put her foot down and concluded that motorcycle riding was no longer for her.

Dad even became a member of the national motorcycle 1,000 mile club--also known in some circles as the "iron butt club." This feat required that you ride your motorcycle 1,000 miles within a 24-hour period of time. He accomplished this motorcycle marathon by travelling to the State of Wisconsin for continuing education. In his own words, "Twice I undertook this challenge by riding a motorcycle 1,000 miles within 24 hours--once out to the University of Madison and another time a return ride with law officers certifying departing and arrival times."

Many days, for years, Dr. Kurtz could be seen riding his motorcycle over the Ashe County roads in his big orange motorcycle suit, leaning with the mountain curves and enjoying every minute of it. He logged thousands of miles in both traveling around the county and over a lot of the country.

From the day Dad arrived to live in Ashe County in June of 1956 until the day he died, April 2010, he had truly found a home in these magnificent mountains. Whether crossing them by foot, bicycle, motorcycle or automobile, he had found a place and a people with whom he could honestly say he had fallen in love.

Over his nearly fifty-four years as a resident of Ashe Pop had climbed most of the county's mountains, medically treated many of her citizens, and crossed a majority of her roads by bike, motorcycle, and automobile. In affirmation of Ashe County and his move south in 1956 Dad concludes, "Orpah and I believe this was an excellent location and home for our own needs and for the raising of our own four loving and lovable children."

Cave on Mount Jefferson

Fat Man's Squeeze

View from summit of Phoenix Mountain

Father and Sons on Holy Mount—Jerusalem 2000

Brutal 100 Bike Ride

Pop in West Jefferson Parade

Water Break

Celebration of 1,000 rides up Mt. Jefferson

Nanny and Pop

Pop and Nanny's 41ˢᵗ wedding anniversary

Dressed for the ride

CHAPTER SIX
THE FINAL CROSSING

"I have fought the good fight, I have finished the race, I have kept the faith. Now there is in store for me the crown of righteousness....." St. Paul, 2 Timothy 4:7-8

For Dad Ashe County was a fit. It was a place to which he had been called. It was a place to which he had been sent. It was a people whom he loved and served. It was home.

Dad reflects, "Dr. Jones had a friend whose life he had saved and in gratitude wished to build a house with a builder-colleague on an available lot two blocks from the local hospital, custom-built for the new young physician coming to town, in honor of Doc Jones. The home was actually located on a street which bore the builders names--Roland-Faw. Living in this home I felt a kinship to the early settler British physician depicted in the nearby Boone, NC drama, 'Horn in the West,' when the early mountain settlers wished to build for this doctor frontiersman a dwelling in their colony! Mr. Roland delighted to show me around the county including the geographic center, Warrensville. While living in this first home the hospital promised to pay $750.00 per month and dining room privileges. They never once deviated from their promise."

Years later, during retirement, Pop penned these lines, "Life in Ashe County entailed three more residences: One on Old Route 16 where we raised our four children, one at the foot of Mount Jefferson from which I rode over 1,000 trips by bicycle up a 3 mile ride to the summit, and finally living in the Mountainaire Golf Course community.

We don't know what our future dwellings will be like but our needs have been well-supplied. We are blessed to have a very comfortable home and a delightful neighborhood and good medical resources with skilled supportive services in reasonable proximity as well as a supportive small church in the 'center of Ashe'--the choice we feel God has provided. We both still serve as volunteers, Orpah faithfully and frequently delivering Meals on Wheels and myself on health-related committees and Hospice-patient visits."

While Pop found a wonderful temporal earthly home his faith was placed ultimately in his eternal heavenly home. This was an eternal hope that he often sang about, frequently meditated upon, and a resurrection hope that motivated and energized his earthly service and living. It was the hope of a new home-- A permanent home. A home prepared by Jesus, as Jesus describes, "Do not let your hearts be troubled. Trust in God; trust also in me. In my Father's house are many rooms; if it were not so, I would have told you. I am going to prepare a place for you. And if I go and prepare a place for you I will come back and take you to be with me that you also may be where I am" (John 14:1-3).

On Monday, April 26th, 2010 Dad made his final crossing….his home going. After eighty-six years of life, after more than forty-seven years of practicing medicine, after more than sixty years of marriage to Orpah the love of his life, after raising four children, after more than 1,000 bike climbs up to the Mt Jefferson summit, Pop was called by his Creator to his eternal home.

Dad had fought the good fight. He had finished his race. He had kept the faith. His reward was received.

On Saturday, May 1st 2010, hundreds gathered in the chapel at Boone Family Funeral Home in West Jefferson, NC for a Christian Service of Death and Resurrection as we celebrated the earthly and resurrection life of Dr. Elam S. Kurtz. The worshipful and celebrative funeral service incorporated a lot of singing, speaking by several pastors, and sharing by family members.

Reflecting upon Pop's life during the funeral Becky shared, "Dad often said, 'poverty is a lack of options, not a lack of wealth.' I used that quote as the theme for a speech I gave as a college student. Dad inspired me to remember to always seek the opportunities in life. Exploring the world; getting to know new people; serving others; experiencing art, theatre and music; continuous learning--all of these were ways to more fully experience the riches of life. Life, for Dad, wasn't about making money. It was about being rich with friends, good health, community, faith, knowledge, and creativity."

Karen added, "Dad was kind and generous. Since his passing, we've heard numerous expressions from his grandchildren and from people in this community of Ashe County--and even from people in other countries--about how Dad's kindness and generosity touched their lives."

Some of these comments to which Karen alluded appeared on the Boone Family Funeral Home website in the form of condolences to the Kurtz family. A sampling follows:

"Dear Orpah and Family, My heart is just broken. I want to let you know that each of you are in my thoughts and prayers. I have been remembering all of the good times I had while working for Dr. Kurtz in the Lansing office. He was always my doctor when I was a little girl and was always so good to me. I'm sure the days ahead will be very hard for each of you, but remember God is there for you and will help you. Love to you all."

"Words cannot express the sadness I feel in my heart. High Country Health Care Hospice lost a wonderful caring volunteer and Ashe County lost a great man. My thoughts and prayers are with your family at this time. He will truly be missed."

"Elam was a great friend to us. He will be greatly missed by all of his friends and especially his church family. He was a great inspiration to us all. We know for a fact he loved the Lord, his family and his church family. My wife and I were blessed to be able to call him our friend."

"There are no words to express what Dr. Elam meant to me and my family. I have known Dr. Elam and his family since I was born. Dr. Elam and I use to laugh about different things. He was so witty. When he delivered me he gave me a pop on the backside as they use to do to make the babies cry and get a good breath. We had fun telling that he gave me my very first spanking. He was my doctor growing up and then my ride to Vacation Bible School at Meadowview Mennonite Church. Along with my sisters, we would sing all the way to church. I remember an Easter Sunrise Service where I stood beside Elam as we sang 'O Happy Day.' I will never forget that. I was very young and he seemed to be the biggest man I had ever seen, but he was the most kind and gentle man I had ever known. Later in years I was blessed to get to work with him at High Country Family Medicine. He would take me to lunch on his motorcycle which was equipped with headphones so that I could listen to music. It was great! He was always so loving and kind to all of his patients and he always thanked me for a job well done at the end of the day. He was the best! He and I stopped working at the same time. I left work to raise my children and he left to continue to bless others with his services. I will really miss seeing him and hearing him at our 5th Sunday singings. He will never be forgotten and he will be missed a great deal! There are so many memories I have that I could write all day and not get them all written down. God has blessed me to have known Dr. Elam and his family. Orpah, Karen, Michael, Becky and Kevin I pray that God will give you peace and comfort. Knowing that your Dad is playing his autoharp and singing in the best choir ever should give you a peace that passes all understanding. He was amazing and loved by ALL who knew him. God bless."

"Dr. Kurtz was my grandmother's doctor for many years up until her death. He always called her granny and she loved her doctor. I brought her back home from Baptist Hospital with Dr. Kurtz's help. They had told me she was going to die. So I called Dr. Kurtz to help me bring her home to die. After she got home and she saw Dr. Kurtz she began improving each day. She lived another 5 years working in the gardens she loved. I also worked with Dr. Kurtz at Emerald Health Care Center where he took care of his patients. He always had a smile on his face and was always willing to listen and help out. He will be missed and not forgotten. Earth's loss is heaven's gain for sure!"

"Elam was my best friend! When we moved to Ashe County in 1980 Elam and Orpah took us under their wings. I rode Mt. Jefferson with him, rode in the Brutal 100, and he hiked me across every mountain in the county. We competed in many various games including chess, ping-pong, etc. He would never let me win despite the pleadings from Orpah. Elam accomplished what he was created for….he glorified God in his life. Our prayers will continue for all of you during this difficult time."

The above written comments as well as many other written and verbal comments, which space does not allow to be printed, were all deeply appreciated by the entire Kurtz Family. This amazing outpouring of love and support reminds us of the many lives which Pop touched and impacted for good.

Continuing with this same theme of Pop's positive influence upon others, Kevin shared the following during The Service of Death and Resurrection, "For 37 years as a solo physician, Dad tirelessly served his patients not only with house calls but often seeing his patients in the hospital not once but twice per day. His office staff, many of whom were with him for most of those years, also played an integral part in his provision of care to the community.

Dad's last day on this earth was Monday, April 26th, and it was like any other weekday for him since retirement. For his retirement in 2003, Ashe Hospital had given him a lifetime membership to their prevention and wellness center, Mountain Hearts, and he had gone there, as he did on Monday, Wednesday and Friday mornings to exercise. Later in the day, he rescued Mom from some car trouble at Wal-Mart, which I know made him feel good, as nothing pleased him more than fixing things for his wife of 60 years. After that, when my wife Beth was occupied at work, he picked up our daughter, Carter, from school and they were able to have a wonderful conversation on the ride home together as grandfather and granddaughter. Just as he approached every day, his last day with us was about service before self.

What a wonderful sharing time we have had as a family during this week. On Wednesday night we as a family had a viewing of Dad in an open casket. What a blessing to have 16 family members gathered and holding hands around his casket, as we cried and prayed, sang and shared stories and then laughed through tears celebrating this remarkable Husband, Father and Grandfather in our lives. Dad's expression then, as it was throughout his life, was one of peace. Dad's signature word with e-mails and correspondences was "Shalom," a Hebrew word used either as a greeting or a farewell meaning "Peace." For me personally, I have lost my father, my mentor in becoming a physician, my chess-playing buddy, and my friend. He encouraged me so much in life and was a man of action not just words. I don't know why God decided it was time to take Pop from us. But what he created in Pop was one of a kind. I guess God just needed another 'great physician' in heaven. Shalom, Pop-- Rest in peace."

* *

As has been mentioned, Dad left this world on Monday, April 26th at a little past six o'clock in the evening. Mom had called him to the supper table but he did not arrive. So, she went to look for him and found him lying on the floor. She called Beth, her daughter-in-law nurse who lived nearby. Beth came as quickly as she could, and did all that was humanly possible, but Pop did not respond. Soon after Beth's arrival the first responders from the local rescue squad showed up, but nothing could be done.....Dad was gone. He died at home.....peacefully.....after having lived another full and productive day.

All four of us children give thanks to God for our final experiences with Pop preceding his death. Kevin, who lives in the same neighborhood as Dad and Mom, made frequent stops at their home to check in with them or to play a game of chess with Pop. Karen and Becky, who live in Atlanta, were blessed to host an anniversary celebration for Mom and Dad and spend several days with them during the month of April.

I also was given a treasured gift of final time with Dad. As a pastor of a church I do not take off many Sundays. Very rarely do I do so. On the days before Dad passed away I spent the entire weekend with Mom and Dad. We spent hours talking, walking, eating meals together, playing table games, and attending Warrensville United Methodist Church together for worship on Sunday morning, April 25th. During this worship service I was privileged to hear Pop sing for the final time in an earthly choir, as he sang a solo, "How Great Thou Art," his favorite hymn! How awesome to hear once again that melodious and strong voice of my Dad, the voice that had been heard so many times before singing the adoration and praises of his Savior and Lord ….. That same voice which had wakened me so many mornings to get up and get ready for school… That same voice which had called me home for supper while playing in the Jefferson neighborhood…That same voice which had affirmed me in my pursuits and decisions.

Sunday, April 25th, 2010 would be the last time to hear Pop's earthly voice singing, for on Monday, April 26th he became a permanent member of the heavenly choir. After an earthly life that was so full and faithful and fruitful, Dad made the final crossing.…crossing over Jordan into the Promised Land through the grace of God's resurrection power through Jesus Christ. In the words of that familiar hymn which Dad had often sung, "When I come to the river at the ending of day when the last winds of sorrow have blown. There'll be somebody waiting to show me the way I won't have to cross Jordan alone.

"I won't have to cross Jordan alone. Jesus died all my sins to atone. In the darkness I see he'll be waiting for me. I won't have to cross Jordan alone."

Following the Service of Death and Resurrection and a subsequent luncheon and sharing time at Warrensville United Methodist Church, the family held a private service of interment at the Warrensville UMC cemetery. Dad's ashes were buried in a grave plot on an Appalachian hill. How appropriate…the man who had crossed over from north to south.… the man who had crossed over the many Ashe County mountains by foot, bike, motorcycle and car.….the man who had found a home in these mountains, was buried on a mountain in the geographical heart of Ashe County! From Dad's burial plot one can see the surrounding mountains, including Phoenix Mountain which he so loved to climb; the church steeple of Warrensville UMC, a church he loved dearly; and a view of Highway 194, the road he crossed for so many years on his daily drive to his office in Lansing from his home in Jefferson. Significantly, the Warrensville cemetery is located half way between office and home…two foundational places where Pop loved and served.

We give thanks to God for loaning us Pop for all these years and for giving us all these experiences and all these memories which we cherish. Shalom, Pop--Rest in peace!

Go Rest High on That Mountain*

I know your life on earth was blessed, serving God and humankind. You served with strength and, oh, such vigor, you gave God body, soul and mind.

Chorus: So go rest high on that mountain

Dad your work on earth is done.

Go to heaven shouting, love for the Father and the Son.

How we cried the day you left us, gathered 'round your grave to grieve, wish I could see the angels' faces as they hear your sweet voice sing.

Chorus

*This song was sung at Dr. Kurtz's funeral.

In Celebration of Life of

Dr. Elam Stoltzfus Kurtz

Saturday, May 1, 2010

ACKNOWLEDGEMENTS

Amanda K. Gross – Cover design

Mrs. Phyllis Rowe – Assistance with graphics and photographs